A Saharan Sketchbook

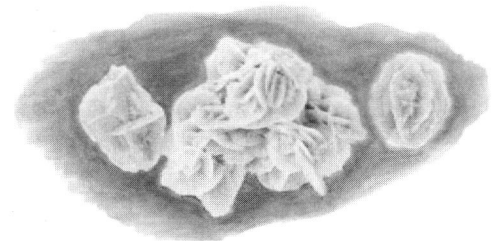

*Formations of petrified sand found in the Sahara and
known as 'Roses of the Sands'.*

The pick-up truck in the Hoggar Mountains.

A Saharan Sketchbook

A MEMOIR OF A JOURNEY IN AN AFRICA OF YESTERDAY

Olivia Willes

Wayfarer

Distributed by Gazelle Book Services Limited
Falcon House, Queen Square
Lancaster, England LA1 1RN

British Library Cataloguing in Publication Data
A catalogue record for this book is available from the British
Library

ISBN 0 9543639 0 6

Typeset by Amolibros, Milverton, Somerset
This book production has been managed by Amolibros
Printed and bound by T J International Ltd, Padstow,
Cornwall, UK

Contents

Part One

Part Two

List of Illustrations

All paintings are by the author.

Olivia sketching north of In Guezzam

Preface

It was 1954 when I took up my job in the British Cameroons. Not a great deal had changed there during the previous century.

Mount Cameroon, over 13,000 feet and the highest peak in sub-Saharan West and Central Africa, dominated the landscape. At its southern foot sat the little town of Victoria.

In 1858 this coastal region was swampy, densely forested and completely devoid of inhabitants. One day in that year a large black canoe approached from the Gulf of Guinea, intending to make a landing. It had on board a Baptist missionary, the Reverend Alfred Saker, and forty-two liberated slaves. They had come from Fernando Po, where Catholicism prevailed. Saker's mission had established a Baptist settlement some distance inland from this coast ten years earlier, and it was to this that he was now bound.

A few months later Saker, a man of enterprise, bought from the Bakweri chiefs a ten-mile coastal strip for his mission, naming it Victoria, after England's queen.

In 1914 the British took over protection of this part of the Cameroons, having been forestalled in doing so by the Germans in 1884. After World War I the whole territory was divided and mandates were conferred, under the League of Nations, to Britain and France.

However, almost all the estates, where the rich, volcanic soil had been cultivated by the Germans, were bought back by them, and remained in their hands until World War II. Thereafter they were administered by the Cameroons Development Corporation (CDC), and the territories were under UN mandate to Britain and France.

In October 1955 I left my job, with the intention of travelling to Algiers overland as part of the homeward journey. It so happened that this was a propitious time for such a project, there being no political instability in the region as yet. Interestingly, too, it turned out that this was, in fact, the end of an era in West Africa.

Niger, where we would enter the Sahara, was French territory, as was the remainder of our desert route.

In 1960 the Federation of Nigeria gained independence, as did Niger. Algeria became independent in 1962.

PART ONE

CHAPTER ONE

An idea takes shape

People who like this sort of thing will find this the sort
of thing they like.

Abraham Lincoln (judgement on a book)

"One way to return home would be via the Sahara," remarked
Peggy, who shared my office.

It was the spring of 1954, and my job was with the CDC in
the British Cameroons.

Peggy's remark seemed to sink in. Memories of my Women's
Auxiliary Air Force (WAAF) service in the Middle East were
still fresh. Latterly, I'd been working with the Forces Broadcasting
Service (FBS) at Kabrit in the Canal Zone, not far north of Suez.
There, apart from having the Great Bitter Lake on our doorstep,
we were surrounded by desert sand. Just visible from the FBS
station were Dakotas parked at RAF Kabrit, with their reflections
miraged. Ever since my time there, I'd felt drawn to return to
hot, arid, sandy places. This was in sharp contrast to most of
my colleagues out there, who felt nostalgic for the green fields
of England.

Finding it difficult to settle down in post-war London, I'd
started to look for something overseas. Eventually, one icy January

day I was interviewed for a job at this tropical outpost with the name of Bota (and hot enough to roast an ox!). The recruiting agent (named Mr Ovens!) offered me the appointment right away with an eighteen-month contract. The passage by banana boat and my arrival here were very recent; it was surely a bit soon to be thinking about my journey home.

Peggy must have sensed my interest in the Sahara. "There's a bus service going across it, too," she added.

I thought about the incongruous bus. It didn't really exist, as I found out later; a company called Transafricaine had at one time attempted to operate some sort of passenger service, but this never came to anything. Anyway, on that day the seed of an idea was planted that lingered on somewhere in the back of my mind, and despite all the obvious obstacles, the non-existent bus gave me something to dream about.

I liked Bota and the Cameroons in general. The scenery was beautiful in a lush and grandiose way. The great volcanic Mount Cameroon provided the backdrop. Bota was the spot on the coast where the headquarters of the CDC, my employers, was situated. There was nothing else to Bota; only the offices, the bungalows provided for the staff and a central clubhouse. There were tennis courts and a swimming pool at the club and sandy beaches within reach, which one could get to on Sundays.

There being no restaurant, entertaining was done at home, lots of it, sometimes quite lavishly, and this was a major pastime. (Single girls took their full share, though rather oddly none at all was expected of single men!)

A few miles distant was Victoria, which had a bank and two shops, one a branch of the United Africa Company and the other a Basel Mission bookshop. Good Swiss watches were obtainable from the latter and the former supplied us with imported food and drink and, with luck, a cotton dress or two when those we'd brought with us were faded and falling apart from wear and tear.

Surprisingly, the climate didn't seem unpleasant and soon one became acclimatised. A fresh sea breeze, peculiar to this bit of the coast, sprang up every morning to relieve the heat and humidity. At ten o'clock it would surge in through our office window – woe betide any documents not weighted down – but it did make the office quite a pleasant workplace. The climate, seemingly moderate, was said to have an insidious effect on the health, however, and the maximum tour of duty was fixed at eighteen months.

The rainy season lasted four or five months of the year and was cool and often sunless; and, like somebody-or-other's advertised salt, when it rained it poured. Nearby in the bush was a place called Debundscha, which was the second wettest place in the world, though why Debundscha should suffer more than elsewhere in the surrounding region is not clear.

Due to the humidity, any garments or shoes not kept continually in our electrically heated wardrobes would soon be destined for the dustbin.

I had a delightful bungalow, with furniture made locally from local timber. The largest item supplied was a sideboard for drinks.

The birds sang marvellously, and I came to know their various calls, without ever finding out their species.

Life at Bota could be summed up as a typical example of British colonial life as it was at that time.

The small banana boats of Elders and Fyffe plied to and fro between Tiko Creek in the British Cameroons and the Liverpool docks. On each trip they carried ten or a dozen passengers, made up of new staff members of the CDC or existing ones coming from or going on leave. Friends made on the outward trip often formed the nucleus of one's circle after arrival. In my case, Margery was one of these, as was Jan. These two, who later became engaged, were among my closest friends at Bota.

It so happened that Jan, a Dutchman, had a cousin who was making his way overland towards this region. I heard his name mentioned occasionally, though he didn't seem to be making much progress, and as time went by we almost began to wonder if he was not a figment of Jan's imagination. Jan, however, was keeping more or less in contact with his legendary cousin. "When you arrive," he wrote, unknown to me, "I'll introduce you to a girl I know so we can make up foursomes."

One day the lone traveller materialised, rather like a visitor from Mars in our circumscribed little community. His name was Pete. I was interested to meet him, as he would be a good source of information of the kind I might need, were I ever to succeed in travelling.

Pete's form of transport, which had brought him all the way from Algiers to the Cameroons, was nothing if not extraordinary. With his luggage in the sidecar, he rode a large and powerful but thoroughly obsolete Zundapp motorcycle, of the kind used in Rommel's desert warfare. It seemed wildly unsuitable for such a long desert crossing. Yet it had got him to his goal (though not without difficulties).

"I need a good rest," he said. "Then I'm going back by banana boat."

Over the next few weeks, I naturally learned a lot about the wonderful things he had witnessed, and also how he'd wished that there'd been someone appreciative to share those solitary experiences. There were countless traveller's tales, some quite awesome, yet almost nothing I heard detracted from my interest in such things.

One day Pete was in reflective mood. "How I'd love to see

again all those places and the many friends I made along the way!" Similarly, he once exclaimed: "How boring that banana boat will seem!"

Hard as it was to imagine anyone wanting to relive such a journey, it almost seemed that an idea similar to the one I harboured had planted itself in his mind too.

Very soon a real plan would begin to evolve.

CHAPTER TWO

Marking time

The White Rabbit put on his spectacles.

Lewis Carroll, Alice's Adventures in Wonderland

My colleagues being late risers on Sundays, I had no difficulty in getting a CDC car and driver for a weekly trip to one of the beaches. There was only one family that sometimes frequented the same beach as I did; otherwise it was likely to be completely deserted. Liking privacy to sunbathe, one day I decided to push my way through some palms, and I found an ideal secluded semi-shaded nook. I noticed as I lay down that the surface of the sand seemed to be peppered with tiny holes, like a pegboard, but I thought no more about it and dozed off. When next I opened my eyes I was surrounded by several hundred frogs, either sitting beside or peeping out of the holes, all eyes seemingly on me! When I sat up with a start, they all popped down the holes, in unison. From then on I looked elsewhere for shady nooks – making sure they were free from any hint of jack-in-the-box frogs or their perforations.

With Pete around I had a ready companion for Sunday outings. Often we packed up picnics and went to one of the beaches for the day. Simon, the driver, was quite contented.

He would go off hunting for iguana. If successful, he could sometimes be seen making a fire and cooking the creature for his lunch.

When swimming, Pete made a practice of wearing his spectacles.

"You shouldn't unless you attach them in some way," I warned; but my words fell on deaf ears. Eventually the inevitable happened: they were lost at sea, and all our searching was in vain. I thought then that the awful inconvenience of waiting while an optician in Holland made a replacement pair and airmailed them to Bota would cure him of the habit. But he was strangely incorrigible.

One day we visited an island, a great hunk of rock a mile or two out to sea. It was inhabited, the only one of the several offshore islands that was, and from Bota the tiny houses of the village were just visible where they huddled on the narrow cliff-top. The villagers came once a week by canoe to the mainland to attend Sunday service at the mission church. They were willing to provide a canoe, at an appointed time, to take us across to the island.

I had never witnessed what went on on this Bota shore, but when I arrived I was more than taken aback. The fresh Bota breeze seemed to have risen to a force-eight gale, with seas to match. Tremendous breakers were crashing against the steeply shelving shore. I was incredulous that a boat could be launched, until I watched and saw that it was possible – for just a few fleeting moments between each monster wave. It was frightening, but I knew the islanders would not take chances.

When signalled, we leapt into our canoe, were pushed out by six helpers, while the oarsmen paddled for all they were worth and we were borne out a safe distance before the next giant came crashing ferociously onto the shore.

On landing, we walked around the village on the island that I had so often looked at with curiosity from my office window. Men sat outside their doorways, making or repairing nets. Fishing was the only occupation, there being practically no soil for cultivation. The lack of soil had driven the villagers to the gruesome expedient of burying their dead under the floors of the houses. For myself, I would not have cared to spend a night there in a village house!

The island children were magnificent swimmers; we could see them body-surfing near the rocky shores below and we suddenly felt like a swim ourselves. We made our way down to the cove where canoes were pulled up on the sand and little black pigs were rooting around. The sandy beach looked safe for bathing, shelving gently and therefore presumably free of barracuda, which inhabited the seas hereabouts and made it unsafe to swim in deep water. Flinging our clothes onto a high rock, well out of reach of the piglets, who obviously had ideas about eating them, we raced into the sea.

Pete was wearing his new spectacles.

"Your spectacles," I yelled, "I can't bear it!"

"Don't worry," he called back breezily, "these new frames fit securely and won't come off."

Next time I looked in his direction, Pete was peering myopically at a group of children who had gathered to watch us. I could just hear what he was shouting at them.

"One pound for any boy who can find the spectacles!"

His words brought a shoal of small boys darting like minnows through the sea. They started diving in the area where he was treading water. I waited helplessly – then after a very few minutes a miracle happened: a tiny arm shot up like a periscope – clutching the spectacles. A pound was a big sum of money to the islanders. I breathed normally again.

At the appointed hour our boatman came to take us back to the mainland. All told, I felt I had had enough excitement for one day, what with that embarkation at Bota, and then the suspense while the spectacles were being sought on the seabed. I was content to relax, as far as was possible in the cramped space of the canoe. As for Pete, he seemed afflicted by an excess of energy. To my horror he plunged into the sea and swam abreast of the canoe. He was certainly aware of the barracuda danger.

I remember being told of an occasion when, in order to get the photo he wanted, Pete had climbed along the branch of an old tree on the edge of a cliff. Margery was horrified. "It might have broken under your weight," she said. "The chances were slight," replied Pete, with a shrug.

It became clear from instances such as these that here was someone not to be deterred by an element of risk as the rest of us might. In trying to assess his suitability as a potential desert companion, I decided that this characteristic was not wholly bad. When it came to the vitally important rules of desert travel, Pete did know his onions and, in due course, he was to make sure that I did too.

It's not uncommon for people to set out together confidently on "adventure" journeys, only to find their friendship under strain when things don't go smoothly. Then comes the point when they have to split up. With our shared enthusiasm and determination the prospects seemed good.

For me, with my wild travel idea, the near impossibility of finding a companion (or companions) had from the start been the likely stumbling block. Anyone suited to the role would be something of a rarity. But that piece of the jigsaw seemed to be falling into place.

Soon my far-fetched pipedream had become a substantive plan.

From all that we heard of his outward journey, we could see that Pete was very capable of dealing with mechanical breakdowns or other problems.

He recounted how, on one occasion, he had arrived at a point where the road was completely flooded and there was no apparent means of getting the motorbike across. To retrace his route and make a detour was out of the question. After arriving at the solution, he unloaded his equipment, unpacked his tools and proceeded to dismantle the entire vehicle. Next he commandeered a herd of cattle that came along to wade across. He attached the components to the cows and, gearbox on one beast, a wheel on another, and so on, he got the motorbike bit by bit to the other side, there to reassemble the whole thing. The task lasted several days altogether.

This picture of my co-driver's attributes fits in well with that of the car we eventually bought. In those rather early days of motoring, cars were in the habit of breaking down at the roadside. One expected it. But no one could have expected what we were in for with the car *we* bought. That had to be experienced to be believed.

CHAPTER THREE

Practical details

"The time has come," the Walrus said,
"To talk of many things:
Of shoes – and ships – and sealing-wax –
Of cabbages – and kings.
And why the sea is boiling hot –
And whether pigs have wings."

Alice's Adventures in Wonderland

If asked to estimate the time we would take, we might have guessed that three months should suffice. In fact we took seven, four months journeying through Black Africa and three in the Sahara.

We planned a route keeping almost entirely to high altitudes and taking us through the northern parts of the Cameroons – British and French – and Nigeria, all regions with a pleasant dry climate. At Kano we would continue northwards via the spectacular Hoggar route, which of the two routes was at the time the more difficult.

It was on this desert route that a party of four young English people travelling in a Morris Minor came to grief and lost their lives. Unfortunately, this tragedy occurred and was in the news while the plan was being formulated, and I suspect gave rise to anxiety and head-shaking among any of our relatives and friends who knew of our project.

The truth was that this disaster arose from causes that could and should have been avoided. The occupants of the car had an insufficient supply of water, had no map with them and had set off from Agadès without first reporting to the French military authorities (who controlled all movements on these dangerous desert routes). This practice of reporting was absolutely essential. When a motorist was authorised to depart from an oasis, a radio message was transmitted to the next one on his route, in this case In Guezzam, giving his expected time of arrival. Should he fail to arrive on time, no action would be taken for two or three days. Then a check would be made with the point of departure to see if he had returned. If, after a further two days there was still no trace, a search would be inaugurated. Failure to report initially was folly.

This party had lost the *piste* (as the desert track was called), though had not wandered far from it. It was easy enough to lose the *piste*. Often blowing sand had obliterated all traces of it. It was quite possible, too, to be led astray by false tracks – left, perhaps, by some army lorry on manoeuvres. If you did lose the *piste*, you had to return quickly while your tyre marks were still fresh to the point where you knew you were on it again; on no account should you attempt any cutting across to regain it.

Should you be broken down, you had to stay with your vehicle, unless you knew that an oasis was within reach; the vehicle could be spotted easily by a helicopter, but you yourself couldn't.

※

As it turned out, the cost of our trip was really very low. This was chiefly because the lifestyle we liked, and which is the best for such a trip, was also the cheapest. Not for us was the style of the deluxe travellers – there *were* a few about – with jeeps fitted with fridges, lots of equipment, and probably servants.

Yet we were not really the rash and improvident itinerants that this story might suggest. We were prepared to give up at any time if need be and fly home.

Nor did we fall into the category of "scroungers". In other words, when we were offered hospitality, we did everything possible to make some return. We did meet some of the "scrounger" types, ill-equipped and often for some reason on their way to visit Dr Schweitzer at Lambaréné – they were just an all-round nuisance.

Pete told of one such individual. He was heading towards Nigeria and asking for advice about routes. Pete suggested a railway that would help him in the direction in which he wanted to go.

"A railway?" exclaimed the man with disdain. "I don't want to *pay*!"

The same individual later declared it to be his intention to ask "the British Consulate in Nigeria" for funds.

"But it's a British territory," said Pete. "The immigration authorities will ask for a deposit from *you* before you can stay there."

"Oh, well," came the reply, "what foreign country could I make for where I will find a British Consulate?"

When we came face to face with the weighty task of choosing a vehicle, our choice was largely governed by price. It was Pete's view that, though ideally it should be with four-wheel drive, an ordinary car was capable of crossing the desert – something new or near new being desirable. (The Citroën 2CV could do it – we met one carrying three people and all their equipment!) With hindsight, I might have shared Pete's view, but only provided Pete himself was to be one of those on board!

In Douala, choice was very limited. Most suitable seemed to be a Morris pick-up truck belonging to a company that had gone bankrupt. It passed such vetting as can be attempted, was only a year old with an apparently low mileage and was alleged never to have been off tarmac roads. It was classed as fourteen English horsepower, which meant limiting our load somewhat. A serious fault was its lack of clearance from the ground; worse still, the lowest point of all was the sump, very vulnerable at the front of the car.

The usual modifications were made (such as removal of the thermostat) and others were thought up and carried out. The torsion-bar suspension system permitted the car to be raised by means of further twisting of the bars. This was very effective, and oversized tyres were fitted on the front wheels to raise it still further.

The car was attractive from the point of view of comfort, and I could see myself surviving the rigours of the life that lay ahead. I liked the well-cushioned bank seat with plenty of leg- and elbow-room. The large area at the back had great possibilities and provided good space for equipment. The light grey bodywork was in very good condition, and the colour seemed to reflect the heat adequately.

The overall appearance was quite impressive, especially after all the rearing up. "Looks a fine car for the job," people said.

Pete carried a complete set of tools; I'm not qualified to specify all that it comprised. It was just a kind of all-purpose wizard's set. It was because these tools came in for such excessive use that our journey took such a long time. It was also why so much of the "kitchen" work landed with me!

Whereas the car and its shenanigans would probably fill an entire book, the subject of what we ate on our travels – ordinary, everyday food – can be disposed of in a few words. Our menu was always the same and the recipe was simple enough, even for the world's worst cook. Ingredients: spaghetti, tinned corned beef, sliced onions and water. Method: boil.

Pete had devised this wholesome dish as his permanent diet during his lengthy motorbike journey, and had found it entirely satisfactory. Therefore I had to learn how to make it. And so, after intensive tuition lasting some sixty seconds, I was able to make it successfully thereafter. It must not be thought that it lacked any variety whatsoever. Although our appetites were good enough to need no titillating, there were some interesting variants. For example, rice was occasionally substituted for the spaghetti, and once in a while I was able to use fresh meat instead of tinned. It was important too that the menu be plentifully sprinkled with Maggi (soy) sauce before being served.

Otherwise we ate whatever was available, but the main meal was always made from this classic recipe, which neither of us ever tired of. It's hard to say why. I don't recollect having any aversion to spaghetti Bolognese, either, after my return to Europe.

Remarkably, I can remember some time later serving "desert hash" (recipe as above) to relatives, who pronounced it to be excellent.

We did like bread for breakfast, and this was the item most difficult to do without. In Black Africa it was generally obtainable in villages, so for the first part of our journey we were OK. There *was* a problem, though, in the French Cameroons, where loaves were made – as in France – long and narrow. This shape was utterly impractical for a tropical climate, of course, and the loaves became hard as pumice-stone in a few hours.

"We've been rather slow," said Pete sagaciously one day, as he wrapped a damp towel round a loaf. "After all, if it's kept moist it can't go hard." At the next meal he unwrapped the bread. True, it was still soft – but it was coated with green mould. We learned many things the hard way.

To make the car into a comfortable dwelling, we fitted removable boards to create an elevated floor and form a large cargo area underneath. The kitchen compartment was under the boards and immediately accessible when the back was dropped. When a real house was needed, our tarpaulin made a tent roof. It was erected in conjunction with removable supports, which were devised for the purpose by Pete. The tarpaulin also served as an overall cover when we were in transit, and it was held down securely with a rope that zigzagged across.

Under the floorboards we had tanks to contain reserve petrol and water, and also, to hold drinking water, a French ten-litre wine bottle in its original basket container. It kept nice and cool in this location and the neck of the bottle protruded through a hole in the boards so that water could be hosed out with a length of plastic piping. Occasionally we drew the hosepipe through the window into the car so we could drink as we went along.

We became very well organised as time passed, everything being streamlined to provide maximum comfort. When we stopped, we sometimes drew off water from the radiator, a source of constant hot water on tap for washing!

There can be little doubt that the timing of our journey was crucial to its success. These were territories destined to "emerge" as independent countries during the next decade, with all the turbulence often engendered by that process. We journeyed through them during an era when the man at the top was European. Like it or not, the indigenous people showed him respect. As for us, when they found we approached them in a spirit of sincere friendship and helpfulness, they reciprocated to the full.

Only one isolated incident took us by surprise. We were passing through a village somewhere in the northern Cameroons when the inhabitants started hurling stones at the car. All we could do was quicken our pace. Then, as we left the outskirts of the village, a woman carrying a shopping basket took one look at us over her shoulder, threw her basket over a fence and proceeded to climb over it herself with such haste that she almost fell to the other side. Something had made strangers unwelcome in that village, but I never knew what.

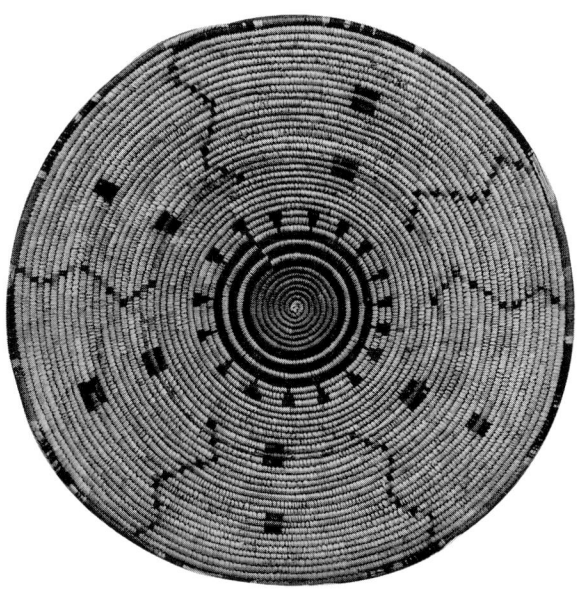

Chapter Four

Life in "a man's world"

"Everybody says, 'come on here'," thought Alice, as she went slowly after it: "I never was so ordered about before in all my life, never!"

Alice's Adventures in Wonderland

Both the long, meandering route that we planned, and our mode of travel, certainly at that time appeared as something rather unusual. Yet presumably there had always been some adventure-seeking men around who, for the sake of the rewards, would ignore the hazards and set off as we did. Men – yes. There's the rub! If a woman participates in such an enterprise she is seen as a kind of nine-days' wonder. That's how it seemed.

Personally, I believed that I could adapt very well to life in male surroundings. What better trial run than those six years in the forces, especially the months I'd spent with Forces Broadcasting at its Kabrit station in Egypt. There I was one of only three girls. We were billeted some miles away, but spent long hours each day at Kabrit. The other two girls each had a boyfriend and I never saw much of them. I preferred to join in group activities with the men during off-duty times, when we'd go to the beach and swim, or in the evening sit in a large tent playing card games. I seemed to be a good mixer and got on very well with everyone. (Any rare attempts at amorous advances were quickly dropped when it was realised that I preferred to be "just one of the guys"!)

What I had yet to learn was that, in the context of my story, the definition of "a man's world" is utterly dependent on nationality. For instance, I discovered that a man's world (French) is nothing like a man's world (English).

Again, in my world, I'd had scant evidence that I created any instant impact on the male libido. However, put me in a French setting and things seemed quite otherwise: a phenomenon that was startling for me. It was not just confined to men isolated in remote places; it was also apparent among those who were settled in communities with their families and friends. A Frenchman who could behave properly when alone in my company was indeed a rarity.

Exceptions occur in both worlds, of course. Such a case was that of one of my fellow-passengers, Adrian, on the banana boat that brought me from England. He and I both sat at the captain's table for meals. Adrian was sometimes drawn in to make up a four at bridge; otherwise he did not take much part in shipboard life.

One night when the voyage was nearly over, we all turned in quite early. My cabin had double doors, an ordinary one and an outer one covered with an opaque mesh, which let air through and kept out insects. It had become so hot that I closed only the mesh door, creating a draught through the cabin, which had a porthole at the other end. The door didn't lock, but in those insouciant days one wasn't in the habit of bothering about locks.

Somewhere between one and two o'clock I was suddenly woken. I switched on the light. There was Adrian – stark naked.

"Hey, you're in the wrong cabin," I exclaimed, with admirable calm.

"No, no. Do put out the light," he said.

I ordered him out very sternly, and he went without much protest, but not before he had carefully put on his clothes, which he'd left in a heap inside my door.

When I sat down to breakfast in the morning Adrian was not at the table. He was frequently late for meals, a habit that had already aroused Captain Long's displeasure, and the only time he'd ever been early for breakfast was on April Fool's Day, when the captain had scared us all by having the gong sounded one hour early.

The men were talking about their dawn trip to the upper deck to watch the wonderful spectacle of the sun rising over Mount Cameroon. This was something habitually practised on this voyage by the more energetic.

"Oh, I'd have loved to see it too," I exclaimed. "I do wish someone had roused me."

I had not noticed Adrian, who had just joined us.

"We would have roused you," proclaimed Adrian in loud and solemn tones, his eyes glued to his plate, "but we were all *much* too shy to come to your cabin."

I'll never know quite how all those men I encountered on the trip saw me. Nor can I grasp how it was that I took on many strange guises; as, for example: bargaining device (Zinder and Tamanrasset), easy game (lots of places), termagant (Bamenda), sex bomb (*partout* – I mean everywhere French!). All added up to a lot of drama.

I had to adjust to a new role, and acknowledge the fact that I was up against a well-organised campaign. It had the semblance of modern warfare – the strategy, the fifth columns, the encircling movements, the reconnaissance raids, the defensive actions, the hand-to-hand battles. It was a full-scale and unremitting campaign, with Pete a bewildered bystander and often an unwitting pawn in the complicated manoeuvres ("You must come on a tour of our workshops/plantations/training centre/oilfields...").

"Didn't you have trouble with all those wild and primitive tribesmen?" I was sometimes asked. Africans, let it be said, behaved with the utmost decorum.

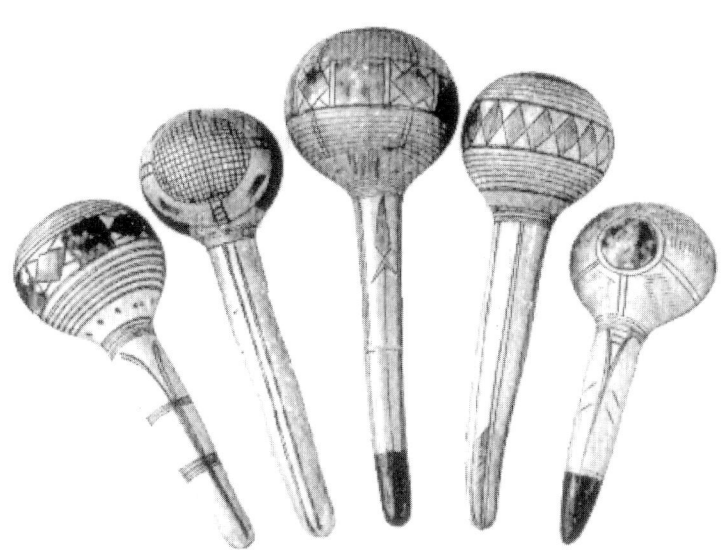

CHAPTER FIVE

Dress rehearsals

"I'm quite content to stay here – only I *am* so hot and thirsty!"

I know what you'd like!" the Queen said good-naturedly, taking a little box out of her pocket. "Have a biscuit?"

Alice thought it would not be civil to say "No", though it wasn't at all what she wanted.

Lewis Carroll, *Through the Looking-Glass*

I worked on to finish my contract. Meanwhile, Pete crossed to the French Cameroons, where there were possibilities of work for him. There he took on a highly ambitious assignment to design and construct a large hangar for a Lebanese-owned sawmill located deep in the heart of the rainforest, some sixty miles to the north of Douala.

There was not a lot I could do in the way of preparations. And there were apt to be hitches. When I ordered an airbed from the department store in Lagos, it arrived promptly by air at our local airstrip. However, upon unpacking, it was found to have the invoice pinned through several layers of the rubberised material!

At this stage it was pretty impossible to estimate what costs lay ahead. What I did know was that I should economise like mad. That, however, was not too daunting, considering there was mighty little to spend money on at Bota (unless you counted alcohol!). One could eat very well, even if imported food was avoided. Locally produced food cost almost nothing, and included beef, which was good and very lean (the livestock hoofed it down from the highlands and had little fat on them on arrival). Delicious things grew locally – paw-paw, corn-on-the-cob, and avocado pear, for example.

I started to "live on the land" and to cut out giving parties, at the risk of seeming inhospitable. Furthermore, pay at Bota was very good. There was also something called a provident fund paid to staff on leaving the CDC. This would provide a very nice "cushion".

As the crow flies, Bota was not far from Douala; yet, to all intents and purposes, it might as well have been 1,000 miles away. There was no link: it was therefore inaccessible – a pity, but one can't change these things.

Pete, for whom there was no such word as "can't", foresaw the need for accessibility. He lost no time in working out a route, albeit a "tough" one, tortuous and involving road, rail and river transport, apart from a lot of foot-slogging along bush paths. With the aid of a map and a native guide, he pioneered it. I was soon to follow in the pioneering footsteps.

A network of narrow-gauge rail tracks, dating from the time the territory was German-administered, gave access to the outlying parts of the plantations. On certain occasions I was to be seen perched beside the driver on a little diesel trolley, which hurtled along the tracks, its rollicking speed slackening only at the approach to junctions where the points were set against us. Then, with great panache, the driver would leap from his seat to race ahead; just in time he would switch the points to the right direction and over I would glide, smoothly and sedately, like royalty in an open landau. Oh so slickly, the driver would catch up again (to my relief) and vault into his seat.

It took one and a half hours to career through the banana groves, the oil palms and the rubber plantations. I was interested to see for myself these plantations, the new housing projects, the brickfield, and so on – places that hitherto had meant no more than names on office files.

It was easy to work at headquarters and never see anything of the actual work of the corporation. When the densely ranked rubber trees with their smooth grey trunks gave way to bush country, the rail track ended, and at that point an obscure little sandy path wound its way into dense bush country.

The little path led to something entirely remote from my working environment. It led to another world.

My first glimpse into this other world was heralded when one day a cable arrived from Pete in Douala warning of his arrival for a two-day visit. I arranged for the little rail trolley to be provided on the appointed evening, and I went myself to meet him.

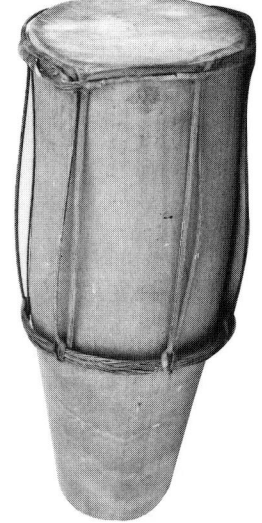

From the end of the railway, I followed the serpentine path and arrived at a river bank, where every so often a canoe appeared, ferrying people to and from the village of Modeka on the far side. I sat down and waited, the short-lived tropical dusk turning into night as I scanned each incoming boatload for Pete. Drums were beating and I wondered what messages they were conveying. As if in answer to my unspoken question, a man who had come along the path behind turned and said, "White master entering the village now." Sure enough, shortly afterwards a call from the ferry boatman reached us out of the dusk and was interpreted for me by the trolley driver standing beside me. There was a white man on board. The white man, one could be certain, was not only footsore but more than ready for the refreshments I had brought along.

Pete told me how helpful the chief of Modeka had been on the day he had left Bota and set out on his original exploration. By way of return, he had asked the chief if he would accept a small present on a future visit – some wine perhaps? No, not wine – what he would like, said the chief, would be whisky or gin.

"I told him about you, and that you might be making the journey yourself some time; and I briefed him to give you all the assistance he could," said Pete. Whereupon I went post-haste to my cupboard and got out a bottle of gin. When Pete was leaving on his return trip, I made *quite* certain that he took the bottle with him for the chief.

Soon it was my turn, and I set off on my first bush trek one Saturday morning. This was an important step, which I regarded as a kind of dress rehearsal; I wanted to prove to myself that I was made of the right stuff, for a lot could depend on it.

Across the river, at the village of Modeka, there was great excitement. "This way, Sister," I was commanded, and was swept along up the hill. "Sister" sounded American, but to Modeka people, apparently, a European woman could only be a nursing sister.

I was led to the chief, welcomed, and a chair was drawn up beside him. Then straightaway I heard the clink of tumblers and gurgling sounds as they were filled. A glass of water would be very welcome. But I was overcome with alarm, realising the dilemma confronting me. The continual boiling and filtering that Bota water underwent was obligatory, and I suddenly saw a glass of the village water as a kind of well-stocked aquarium for microbes. Yet it would be most ill-mannered to decline the offer of a drink.

But there was no need for alarm. (Or maybe there was?) No water this – it was neat gin!

My protests ignored, two well-filled tumblers were set before us. We managed to keep the conversation going and, eager not to offend, I sipped away. The chief brought out to show me what was obviously a greatly prized possession and the envy of all who saw it. This was a gilded cage about four inches high, inside which a lemon-yellow bird perched on a revolving dais. Closer inspection revealed it to be a clock, though reading the time was none too easy. It was the sort of thing popular in continental souvenir shops, and had probably been given to the chief during the time of the Germans.

A guide was commandeered to escort me on my way, and the chief gave me a carved bamboo cane to hand to the chief of the next village, Mungo, as a kind of passport. Despite – or perhaps because of – the quantity of gin imbibed, I made short shrift of the arduous two-hour walk. The centre of an animated accompanying platoon, I must have galloped along. My guide, and everybody else, seemed to have seven-league boots and I felt compelled to keep up. Some of my escorts dropped out when we came to a ford. I sloshed heedlessly through the river. The water came up to my knees, but it came well up the thighs of my companions.

The numbers in the platoon were swelled by inhabitants of one or two hamlets along the way, where it always seemed

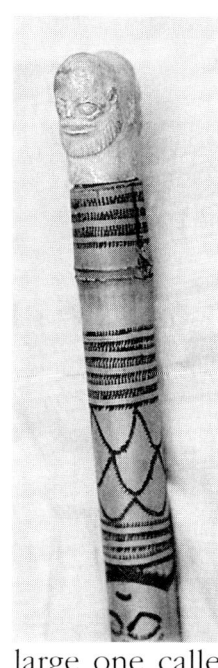

my approach was expected. In a remarkably short time, we arrived in Mungo village.

At Mungo I formally presented the bamboo cane to the chief, who ordered a canoe – actually a hollowed out tree trunk – to be provided for the next stage of my journey. This was a trip down the river that formed the frontier. As I sat in my tree trunk, my gondolier paused a couple of times in his singing to point to some reeds and say cheerily, "Crocodile!" I looked and saw nothing much except, perhaps, some logs floating. Swept along downstream by the fast-flowing current, it seemed only a short way to my point of disembarkation on the French bank, which was yet another native village, a large one called Bwadibo. Close by ran the main north-south road, on which it was easy to get a lift to Douala.

In Bwadibo I came across a French couple. They lived in a simple thatched native house and he was an artist, though he earned his living as a tailor. I realised how pampered we were; by comparison, we lived like lords, and there was something refreshing about this glimpse into a totally different way of life for Europeans in a tropical country.

Douala was a modern city with all the accompanying amenities. Lacking the breeze enjoyed by Bota, it was unpleasantly hot and everything was exorbitantly expensive. Pete was there to meet me at a pre-arranged place, and we made our way to the Hotel Lido. A middle-aged French matron presided at the reception desk. (This was the formidable Madame Museau, who lent her name not to a rose but, as shall be seen later, to a coffeepot.) Cheap, and *just* good enough, the Lido was a hotel used chiefly by French *transporteurs*, the men who spent their time endlessly driving long-distance juggernauts, saving the high earnings this yielded to set themselves up in life.

Douala was no place for anyone who was trying to economise. There was a still cheaper hostelry that Pete had explored. I never heard its name. He viewed it with disdain and referred to it as the "cheap-curtains-hotel". Apparently curtains took the place of walls for the purpose of separating one guest from another. There were no frills at the Lido either, but it was adequate and, even if the rooms lacked some refinements, they did have four sound walls.

I looked around the room and my eye fell on a notice on the wall. It bluntly forbade *célibataires* to bring in native women. Why only bachelors, I wondered vaguely? As for Pete, he was absorbed just then in contemplating the extraordinary bed.

It was quite startling, being of concave form within its frame, and sagging as deeply as any hammock ever sagged.

"Perhaps what we need is a board of some sort…" I mused; whereupon Pete started wrestling with, of all things, the wardrobe door. "Wait – I wouldn't care to get on the wrong side of that fierce-looking manageress," I added uneasily. But Pete had already lifted the heavy door from its hinges. Placed crossways at hip level, beneath the mattress, the wardrobe door served admirably to hoist the whole sorry thing and form quite a comfortable bed.

It is the only time I have ever slept on a mirror.

On the homeward journey next day I was invited to tea with my Bwadibo friends before embarking on the river stage of the trip. They also helped me in arranging the hire of a canoe, and together we chose an intelligent-looking boatman.

After a very short time on the river I realised how slow progress was when going upstream and how much more advisable it would have been to have two oarsmen instead of one. After a while we met a canoe coming downstream with a "nightgown-clad" Hausa trader as passenger. A discussion between the two boatmen ensued and then they drew the canoes into calmer waters among reeds remarkable for their resemblance to yesterday's "crocodile" reeds. The Hausaman's bundle (contraband?) was exchanged for my bag (French cheese), and then I understood: the passengers too were to be trans-shipped. This enabled the boatmen to return to their respective villages, and the total of their efforts would be halved. I was less keen on the idea when I summed up my new boatman. His linguistic abilities were nil (and there was no indication that his IQ was much better). This up-river inhabitant knew no English or French at all.

It started to drizzle. I wondered whether accurate instructions as to my destination had been passed on – for all I knew, there were other villages apart from Mungo.

The rain got heavier. I found an old calabash and baled around my feet. On the impenetrable banks creepers mounted giant mangrove trees and fell again to the water in twisted, knotted ropes. Monkeys chattered. It even seemed that dusk was descending on the primordial scene. The interminable time we were taking and the fact that I recognised no landmarks worried me; there were several forks in the river and I knew that Mungo lay a short way downstream on one of them. At any wrong destination I'd of course be completely lost, and I tried shouting "Mungo" above the incessant chanting. However, as this was the name of the river as well as the village, the boatman's grins of agreement weren't much consolation.

I was not lost and I did get to Mungo eventually. Feeling stiff, but jumping ashore thankfully, I shot down the familiar path in the hope of getting away unnoticed. I took a wrong turning and found myself in a clearing face to face with a group of monkeys who played on white tombstones, eerie-looking in the dim forest light. (When recounting details of my journey to Pete, he interrupted, before I got to this part, with the remark: "I'll bet you went to the tombstones!") I got onto the right path at last, where I collected the usual crowds, chattering and offering to sell me commodities ranging from monkeys and parrots to nuggets of gold. The crowds were welcoming though; once I caught the words "Mammy dropped her handbag." "Mammy" was their distortion of "madam". I turned to see my sou'wester (old-fashioned rain hat) hanging from an outstretched arm.

It was always Sunday night when I passed through Modeka. Most people were attending services being held in the five churches of the village, all of different sects. A sixth service was conducted in a hall where a small group of Jehovah's Witnesses used to gather.

The last stage in this homeward trek involved being guided from Modeka to the nearest dwelling on the plantations, from where a telephone call could be made to obtain a rail trolley. With this last bit, the journey did become somewhat exhausting. But I nevertheless relished the sense of achievement: I was now a real "explorer", and in my new role I had to forget about my physical tiredness.

CHAPTER SIX

To the forest of Loum

On the coast of Coromandel
Where the early pumpkins blow,
In the middle of the woods
Lived the Yonghy-Bonghy-Bò.
Two old chairs, and half a candle, –
One old jug without a handle, –
These were all his worldly goods.

Edward Lear, "The Courtship of the Yonghy-Bonghy-Bò".

In October I was due to leave Bota. This meant a wait in the wings for me. Pete was still at work on the hangar, so the only course at this stage was for me to go and join him at his forest hideout and kill time till our departure. Killing time is a horrid idea, but that is what it amounted to for me, as I really had nothing to occupy my time in the forest.

I crated up my belongings for the CDC to send home for me, keeping very little to take with me. The bulkiest item in my hand luggage was a super tarpaulin that the shipping department had made for me.

Friends and colleagues gave me a very nice send-off. Kathleen, my next-door neighbour and Steve, who were newly-weds, gave me a parting present that was to prove totally invaluable, a foam-rubber cushion. From other friends who were particularly concerned about my welfare I received a wonderful present, a beautiful brass naval compass.

There was a launch going to Douala from the nearby port of Tiko that could take a passenger: I was in luck, for this was a rare occurrence. Kathleen and Steve had just moved to Tiko; they were wonderful, putting me up and getting up at four-thirty in the morning to see me to the launch.

The voyage didn't last long; formalities at the port on arrival took longer. How cumbersome, I thought, in comparison with my new-style bush travel!

Pete was ensconced in a roughly constructed bush-house that stood on stilts in a clearing and overlooked the sawmill. The clearing was steamy and mosquito-ridden – a microcosm of the whole unhealthy world that made up the white man's grave of legend. From the nearest railway station, the place was approached by a mud road that was all but impassable. It was this grim setting and the trapped feeling it inspired in the visitor that made the house such an undesirable residence.

I had never been able to absent myself from Bota for long enough to pay a visit to Loum, as this place was called, and discover for myself what mud, mosquitoes and mugginess can really be like. Pete was anxious about what my reactions would be. When I arrived at Loum station, having left my heavy baggage in Douala to be picked up according to a prearranged plan, he was unable to meet me. Indeed, he was hardly able to walk at all due to a leg injury caused by a falling beam. How he recovered so quickly in that dreadful setting, where every mosquito bite turned septic, and without proper medical attention, was little short of a miracle.

With the help of a Lebanese couple (the only non-Africans living in Loum village), to whom I was wordlessly escorted from the station by a platoon of the kind I was already accustomed to, a boy was rounded up to guide me to the sawmill.

The road wound through a jungle forest; at least, it was not so much a road as a five-mile ribbon of ploughed-up, squelching mud. Like Venice, it was something that had to be seen to be believed – it can't be adequately described. The boy managed to carry my bag and at the same time move like a miniature Nijinsky. I was more like a windmill as I strove to keep my balance, placing my feet insofar as possible in the imprints made by the boy. At least four times I fell and rolled in the mud and, before reaching the house, I had to bathe in a river to remove layers of the stuff.

So much for the road. The house was far less remarkable: it was just a model of how not to build a house. No two pieces of timber matched in any way and it looked as though it had been put together roughly from odds and ends left over in the sawmill – which as a matter of fact was just about what had happened. One got used to the untrimmed ends of timber that protruded all over the place.

The house did run to windows, though there were no such refinements as glazing. These openings were covered by the lowering of square shutters that fitted where they touched. A few days after my arrival a shutter fell from its hinges. I persuaded Pete to replace it with some other bit of wood, as I found it made an excellent drawing-board. So it should, for it was a smooth square of obeche, the wood that is imported from West Africa for the specific purpose of making drawing-boards!

Pete's hangar, his own creation from blueprint stage onwards, was nearing completion. At regular intervals I was taken on a tour of inspection, dutifully making suitable sounds of wonderment and admiration at the precision in the alignment of the beams. I had to regard the structure from many different angles and was regaled with accounts of the engineering feats that had been performed without any of the usual facilities: for example, the means he had devised for hoisting into place the heavy girders that had first to be constructed on the ground, a task normally needing a crane. To add to his difficulties, he was provided with only a handful of unskilled men, though he needed a much larger workforce. Even to a layman it was clear that the whole thing was an astonishing achievement.

We were not quite without neighbours, for there was another small house close by, which was occupied by young men of the Lebanese family who owned the forestry business. Provided it was *en masse* (not otherwise where I was concerned!), the sociability they offered was welcome.

The eldest son was called Nazi and it was Nazi who managed the sawmill on behalf of his father Aziz, who owned it. He was called Aziz Hajj because he had made the pilgrimage to Mecca. Aziz himself never left the main family homestead, which was in Douala. Nazi had an exuberant personality, whereas the other brothers (how many there were I forget) were all rather nondescript. I don't know what they all did. They just came and went with Nazi as aides of some kind.

We seldom saw the womenfolk, as they spent most of their time at home in Douala. Once or twice they came to the forest, and then they stayed at another house, a much larger one, standing in isolation several miles further along the mud road. I thought ours was in the back of beyond until I visited this other house.

The women of the family wore nothing but black, their crêpe dresses making them look older than their years.

They were very neighbourly and we were invited to stay at the house in the back of beyond, where we were generously entertained for three days. Nazi took us in his jeep into the virgin forest in the tracks of a bulldozer right to the point where it was breaking new ground. There was delight at that moment, as an enormous mahogany tree had just been located. Two kinds of mahogany grew in this forest, one of them much more valuable than the other. Only when felled would its type be revealed, and therefore suspense reigned until that moment.

It was very spectacular, but with an awesome beauty that oppressed rather than uplifted; one felt dwarfed beside such trees and almost compelled to speak in undertones. We realised that what *we* knew as rainforest was not at all the real thing. Of course, the huge trees from near the road had all been felled, so that it was bordered by a region of smaller, less valuable ones and jungle undergrowth.

One member of this family, a cousin who had recently arrived from Lebanon, was distinctly unusual. He must have had a name. But I christened him Hashish on account of his air of dopiness, and for us Hashish he remained. Although he was almost always there whenever there was sociability, he could hardly be called a sociable person, for on these occasions he just sat with an amiable, faraway look on his face, hardly ever speaking. But one day all this changed. The conversation had somehow turned to the subject of narcotics, when all of a sudden Hashish came to life. In fact, he became extremely loquacious. All other conversation ceased as Hashish embarked upon an eloquent dissertation on narcotic drugs and the plants from which they are extracted, furnishing his listeners with names and details of particular plants native to the region we were in. That was all – at the end he lapsed into his usual silence.

There was an elderly Frenchman called Monsieur Vermont who worked at the sawmill in the capacity of accountant and office administrator. He had no family, living alone in a bush house half a mile outside Loum village at the side of the mud road. He drove in his jeep each day to the sawmill, where he had a small office. We both liked Monsieur Vermont very much and he used to come with Pete to the house for morning coffee.

Monsieur Vermont was courtly and cultured; he gave the impression of being left over from an earlier age and now moving among strangers. He had an air of elegance despite his shabby bush clothes. In my presence he never talked about his past life, but he once told Pete a little of his history.

Long ago in France he had married. He wanted a wife and family and chose as his bride a young girl, intelligent and good-looking. The girl's parents highly approved of the match.

A shock was in store. After the wedding a scar on his wife's body revealed the truth that had been kept from him – that they would never be able to have children. He placed the entire blame for concealing this fact on the girl's parents. Did the girl share with her parents responsibility for the deception? Or was she herself an innocent victim of secrecy? We never knew; nor did Pete learn how the story ended. It was clear, however, that Monsieur Vermont had lived in solitude for very many years.

Up to the time of my arrival Pete had had meals with the Lebanese men. Now we catered for ourselves, a boy who worked for us bringing our provisions daily from Loum. Having absolutely nothing else to do, I was glad enough to have at least some housekeeping and cooking, though this wasn't easy. Rudimentary furniture and a fridge were supplied in our house, but nothing else. There was also a battered little aluminium coffeepot, abandoned by its former owner and being used by Pete to boil water on his primus. I could have passed the time usefully in concocting simple meals, if only there had been some kitchen utensils in the house. But the tantalising thing was that there were, in abundance – but they were so near and yet so far! For right before our eyes, if we crouched and shone a torch through the slatted door of a barricaded room, an abundance of excellent household and kitchen utensils came into view. I naturally suggested that we might get their owner's permission to use them. "They belong to Madame Museau, the manageress of the Hotel Lido," said Pete, as though that settled the matter. Remembering the forbidding countenance of Madame Museau, I did not pursue the idea.

One day, after due deliberation, we helped two or three already shaky nails holding the barricade to fall out. The door swung open, we entered our Aladdin's cave and helped ourselves to treasures that gleamed as brightly as pots and pans. We picked things that could come to no harm, justifying our actions as we did so with arguments of excellent logic. No one else in our position would leave such sorely needed things in disuse. It wasn't as if there were any possibility of their owner coming to the house either – not in the rainy season anyway, with the road as it was; and what the eye doesn't see.... We argued for a long time, both in the same direction, ending as we had begun, in complete agreement.

Time passed and one day I was preparing lunch when Pete rushed up to the house.

"Madame Museau," he gasped, and the shock of hearing that name made me drop the pineapple I was peeling. We had made jokes of this type from time to time and, simply because anything else would be unthinkable, I decided now it was a joke.

"Madame Museau," he repeated. Something in his voice told me he wasn't joking and I turned to see his face ashen, his unsteady hand clutching a hammer and nails. It appeared that a jeep in which the redoubtable lady was travelling was at that very moment coming round the last bend into view of the clearing. Nazi had known of her impending visit, but hadn't chanced to mention it beforehand.

All of a sudden what had seemed a harmless prank, mere childish mischief, took on a sinister aspect: the mere proximity of that jeep had transformed us into criminals about to be caught red-handed. For a minute I was paralysed with sheer terror! It really seemed futile even to try to round up the loot spread around in a short space of time. But try we did.

As luck would have it, the jeep skidded in the terrible slime at the corner of the road; it made a revolution of 180 degrees and had to be righted before it could complete the remaining fifty yards. This took time.

It was after a lapse of several minutes that a form of ample proportions passed our window, causing a partial solar eclipse in the house that seemed like a prognosis of impending disaster. But, believe it or not, the knock on the door just afterwards occurred simultaneously with Pete's last hammer blow on Aladdin's door.

Pete advanced to greet Madame Museau, wearing his particular cordial and relaxed smile that seldom failed to charm the fair sex. As for me, I also managed a welcome; with words ringing with insincerity, I expressed my pleasure at her surprise visit and regretted that the mud had made her journey so difficult. While I was talking Pete was convulsed with an attack of coughing, which I suspected was a disguise for hysterical laughter.

I had always cursed the mud. That day I loved it dearly.

From this little episode, with its ending more like fiction than fact, a moral could be drawn to give encouragement on occasions of catastrophe such as we were to experience on our travels – something on the lines of: However hopeless the situation may seem, never give up – a stroke of good luck can still keep disaster at bay!

But the most memorable thing about Madame Museau is that for us her name became a household word on account of her coffeepot. Ancient and battered though it was, it was very sound and for seven months on the road it served as our pot-cum-kettle, as prized an object as any valuable heirloom. Once Madame Museau's coffeepot was actually stolen, but I espied this outrage taking place and retrieved the treasure after giving chase deep into the bush. We would have been lost without it.

Chapter Seven

Final preparations

"I wish *I* could manage to be glad!" the Queen said.

"Only I never can remember the rule. You must be very happy, living in this wood, and being glad whenever you like!"

"Only it is so *very* lonely here!" Alice said in a melancholy voice...

Through the Looking-Glass

Pete had to make several trips to Douala and, except when it was absolutely necessary for me to go too, I stayed behind in the horrid house in the steamy clearing.

During these periods of solitary confinement I woke up each morning with the knowledge that the day ahead would be a blank. The boy would come with provisions and I would make him a shopping list for the next day and, after cleaning the house, he'd go home. Monsieur Vermont would come as usual and have coffee with me at mid-morning. Otherwise there was nothing. The sensation of such total emptiness was something I had never experienced anywhere else.

In retrospect, it's surprising that I didn't amuse myself, even at Loum, with some sort of drawing. In those days I needed motivation. Only if some exciting subject presented itself would I be inspired to draw or paint.

Nor was I in the habit then of having a sketchbook always to hand for making hasty scribbles. More's the pity – considering some of the things that might have been recorded along our route during the months that followed.

With no radio, there was nothing to punctuate the hours, and after work stopped at the sawmill and the workers had gone home there was total silence. I'd become so used to the humming of mosquitoes that I hardly heard them.

I'd managed to find some paperbacks in Douala, exhausting the stocks, but they were thrillers of the most trashy kind. One would have to be desperate to read some of them. I was and I did.

Apart from the trash there was Dale Carnegie's *How to Win Friends and Influence People*. It was all right, but just then instructions on how to repel might have been better. The flimsy door did have a lock but this was rather pointless considering that there was a two-foot gap between the outer walls of the house and the roof.

We saw little of the local populace, but African discontent in this territory was already fermenting and Loum Chantier (which was one stop down the railway line) had recently been the scene of the first rioting and incidents against Europeans, troubles that later spread to Yaoundé, the capital. All Europeans were feeling a tiny bit wary.

The length of Pete's absences in Douala was always undetermined; all I ever knew was that after a few days he would arrive at the station on a late train and would come from there on foot, arriving at dead of night. The worst of the rains being over, one could now walk from the station without great difficulty. I insisted that, to warn of his approach, he must whistle some prearranged tune. This he promised to do and the tune decided upon was *God Save the Queen*.

While alone I did have calls from one would-be visitor, the least expected of all – Hashish. However, when told repeatedly that I was too busy to receive anyone, Hashish accepted this unlikely contingency and thereafter the days and nights passed without incident. Even so, I'm sure no patriot heart ever warmed to the strains of the national anthem with more enthusiasm than mine did as I heard those faint, fragmented bars gradually coming into earshot in the small hours of the morning.

Our bush house did not qualify for a postal address, but Loum must have run to a post office of some sort and we were able to have mail sent to us. This was collected by Nazi and brought to us from time to time. Our mailing address was "c/o Aziz Hajj, Loum, French Cameroons", and I fear it seemed rather odd to people at home who had seen me leave to take up work with British administrative authorities.

One day Pete received a mysterious letter, but at the time he didn't mention who it was from. Then one November day we were going to Douala together when he referred again to the letter and mentioned that he had an important shopping commission to carry out.

"I wrote to Arab friends in Agadès telling them I was coming back," he told me. "Now I've had a letter from old Abdul Ahmed. It's about a most urgent request."

I was mildly curious to know what this request could be.

"Although Abdul is an important personage," explained Pete, "he has little contact with the outside world. He hears mention of things that can be obtained in the cities, but I am the only person he knows whom he can ask to get him some."

"Some?"

"Well, you see, it's terribly important to him. Abdul is rich, he has everything he wants and lots of wives, but he's most distressed – he's no longer the man he once was." Pete went on to explain that Abdul had heard about aphrodisiacs that might restore his failing powers, and had set his heart on getting hold of something of the kind. "I'm afraid they may not help in his case," said Pete, "but they're harmless things."

Nice as it would be to help, I wasn't too sure about it. "They may be harmless, perhaps; but they might be abused if they fell into the hands of rotten, unscrupulous types," I suggested.

"Abdul's genuine enough. I can't let him down," replied Pete, who proceeded to show me Abdul's letter. It was a *cri de coeur*. "Aidez-moi, je vous prie. Je suis en panne," it ended up. We couldn't leave Abdul in his broken-down state without giving all possible assistance to remedy it.

So a small package containing an aphrodisiac preparation called yohimbine was purchased in Douala and tucked away in the packing until such time as it could be delivered by hand in Agadès.

At the museum in Douala a talented French artist called Hervigo was exhibiting gouache paintings of the North Cameroons. This gave me the idea of taking gouache with me in addition to oils. They proved very suitable. Only pastels might have been better – quicker and more lightweight – but at the time I was too inexperienced to know.

On leaving the exhibition we called on one of Pete's acquaintances who was helping with the negotiations about the car. His name was Monsieur Bouvier and he was a dentist. Keen to equip myself for the new medium, I asked Monsieur Bouvier whether he happened to know of a supplier of artists' materials. He was ready with an answer, though with his mind on the subject of the car, he had jumped to the wrong conclusion.

"Oh yes, I can direct you," Monsieur Bouvier assured us. "My cousin is an artist."

We followed the directions he gave us and arrived, not at a shop but at the studio of an artist. The artist himself was there in the doorway to greet us.

"My cousin, Monsieur Bouvier, has already telephoned to say you were on your way," he said, "and I would be delighted to paint whatever you choose on the car."

Realising the misunderstanding, we had to explain that we had no thoughts of having maps, place-names, slogans and the like painted on the bodywork of the car.

More than once when on the road we passed vehicles broken down, their sides emblazoned with details of over-ambitious programmes. One such car, elderly and looking like a write-off, was being towed back to Kano from the outskirts on the very day it had set off.

Happily, the artist was able to direct us to an art shop where I could get everything I needed.

The rainy season was coming to an end and the mud road had now improved sufficiently for us to be able to take the car home and use it. Not many days later we were driving down the road when disaster struck; more precisely, a sharp bouncing stone did, hard enough to knock a star-shaped hole in the sump. This being made of aluminium, repairing it wasn't easy. But they were able to carry out an elaborate – and costly – operation in Douala.

❦

We thought of all those sandy tracks we'd encounter in days to come, with rocks and stones concealed in high central ridges, and we wondered if anything could be done to prevent a repetition of the disaster. Following this racking of our brains, there emerged Pete's first Heath Robinson device.

He got to work with a solid sheet of iron, from which he fashioned a large protective shield. This was then suspended, by means of nuts and bolts, to the underside of the chassis to protect the all-too-vulnerable sump, which was not only the lowest but also the foremost part under the car.

"La serviette hygiénique," someone once called this contraption. Albeit an unpleasing metaphor, it was apt. Judging by the knocks and dents it suffered along the way, the object served its purpose very well. However, it was heavy, and because of this it was eventually jettisoned somewhere south of the Sahara. Fortunately the sump never again came to grief, though it was subsequently kept brightly burnished by constant contact with ridges of Sahara sand.

When Pete bought me a bunch of purple grapes as a present, I guessed that his work was deemed to be finished and he had received payment from Aziz. That meant the time of departure was near.

There remained some final touches to be carried out on the hangar, but with instructions written out by Pete, this could be done by others. We loaded the car and got on the road without a minute's delay. It was mid-December.

Monsieur Vermont had not been seen for several days, and just before we left word reached us that he was not well. Before we pulled out of the mud road for the last time we stopped at his house. We found him in bed. At the best of times he looked frail and one felt that, despite all the advances in tropical medicine, the long years spent on the West African coast, unbroken by any home leave, had taken their toll on his health. Now that he was laid up, he looked very gaunt and ill.

Monsieur Vermont did not tell us the nature of his illness,

and we thought it better not to enquire. After a little while we said goodbye and took to the road, two excited people bounding with health and vitality, and it was sad to leave the old man lying all alone in his dark, silent and sparsely furnished room in that inhospitable setting.

CHAPTER EIGHT

Christmas in Nkongsamba

"Very uncomfortable for the Dormouse," thought Alice;
"only, as it's asleep, I suppose it doesn't mind."

Alice's Adventures in Wonderland

The first town on our route was Nkongsamba, and as we headed
north towards it, it was a joy to climb gradually into the hill
country, leaving behind the closeness and clamminess, the rickety
house, the boredom and the mosquitoes.

The Morris was certainly very comfortable. It was well sprung
and the seat was really cushy and roomy. As for the engine, it
was as silent as a sewing machine, which made for restfulness.
Once, at a later date, when our horn failed to work, I remember
seeing a cyclist meandering along a remote bush road. Only
when we were almost upon him did he become aware that a
noiseless monster was behind. He dismounted in terror and
ran for his life, throwing his unfortunate bicycle into the bush
as he did so.

As we entered Nkongsamba, the engine was not silent. There
was a knocking. It was not getting less either, it was increasing.
Steady and mechanical, we couldn't ignore it. With our hearts
sinking into our boots, we knew we must stop at once.

"I think it's a *bielle* that's gone," said Pete with unusual gravity.

"That's a 'big end' in English," I said with commendable slickness (and was never 100 per cent believed). Not that I had ever heard of a *bielle*; I didn't even know what the function of a big end was, but I knew that it could knock and "go" and that when it did these things it was spoken of in hushed tones of great solemnity. Awful and extraordinary as this happening was, at least it served as a forewarning of the kind of things we were going to be up against.

Pete took out the big end that caused the knocking, and I was left in no doubt then what this object was. Space for the lengthy work was provided by the helpful Monsieur Lambert, who operated a metal workshop just outside the town. We resigned ourselves to spending Christmas in Nkongsamba, and some fragments that didn't look their price were rushed from Douala. To be precise, they were *coquilles*, literally "eggshells", but I don't know to this day if these linings for big ends are called eggshells, or something else, in England. Then, and in the months following, I acquired a useless accomplishment: a French vocabulary that, as far as internal combustion engines are concerned, was almost inexhaustible.

Although we were not yet at a very high altitude, we had climbed sufficiently for the air to be much drier and fresher, a fact that alone made our sojourn in Nkongsamba as beneficial as a holiday.

Nkongsamba, the terminus of the railway and the end of the tarred road, was just developing into a modern town. Many of the indigenous population, so recently denizens of a backward area, were still very much newcomers to modernity and all its trappings. Young men over-anxious to appear emancipated made a point of carrying briefcases even if they had nothing in them, and to look erudite they wore spectacles of plain glass purchased in the market. The ambition of any youth was to get a motorcycle, and if he did, before anything else, he removed the silencer.

Even the wearing of shoes could seem an irksome necessity, as was illustrated by an incident that occurred in Nkongsamba at that time. One cinema featured the exciting *Zorro*, a series that always played to a full house. One week's episode was so thrilling and so realistic that at the moment when the band of villains galloped on horseback straight towards the camera, opening fire as they did so, the entire audience rushed for the exits. Soon there was not a soul left; the hall was empty – save for 200 pairs of shoes.

The Lamberts rented their bungalow from an African. His job was that of post-office clerk and, as conditions were the same for local recruits and French expatriates, he drew the pay and family allowances of the French civil service. The fact that he had twenty-two children meant that he was a comparatively well-off young man. By the time new bungalows he was building were completed, he would be better off still.

Madame Lambert did the cooking and most of the housework herself. The bungalow, though beautifully kept, was not particularly modern or labour-saving. The shower, which we were invited to make use of, was little more than a bucket of water that overturned when a string was pulled.

One evening just before Christmas we arrived at the Lamberts' to find a heated argument in progress. A man, whom I shall call Monsieur X, had come to ask for assistance with his car, which had broken down nearby.

Monsieur X was a young African and a parliamentary candidate in the forthcoming elections (he was in time to become a well-known politician). The Lamberts had visitors and it was clearly difficult for them to help just then. The visitors were listening to the argument that had developed and were joining in with great zest. Tempers started flaring all round. Whatever the actual gist of the argument, I noticed that Monsieur X was coming in for a lot of slanging, with the use of *tu* and *toi*. Neither a loved one, a child nor an animal, nor considering himself as belonging to a subject race, Monsieur X was flinging back *tu* and *toi* as if they were boomerangs. Only Pete's willingness to get the broken-down car going again brought the scene to an end.

The trouble with Monsieur X's car was located in the battery. Pete got the car going with jump leads and our battery, for which Monsieur X was very grateful. As a mark of his gratitude, he invited Pete and me to dinner. An evening was fixed to fit in with his strenuous programme in the election campaign, which was occupying a great deal of his time, involving as it did much touring round the countryside.

Monsieur X entertained us in his smart little bungalow. A good meal had been prepared and was served by an indeterminate number of brothers and cousins who hovered in the background throughout; and during the evening a smiling but shy Madame X was brought in very briefly from the kitchen to meet us. After dinner we sat in comfortable chairs and talked, and a tray of coffee was placed on a low table in front of our host. We'll never forget what happened next.

The conversation suddenly trailed off and we came to realise that fatigue was having its effect on Monsieur X, for he had fallen fast asleep. Time passed – twenty minutes, thirty.... We were at a loss to know what etiquette required that we should do. To slip away might appear rude; yet if we sat on and on, our host's embarrassment on awaking might be considerable. A brother, who seemed to view our dilemma rather lightly, volunteered to transmit a thank-you note, should we decide to leave.

The best part of an hour had elapsed and it looked as though the situation might continue for the rest of the night. We started to write our note. But wait… I nudged Pete and he put away his pen. Our host had moved and was leaning forward. He was once again with us. With a steady hand and his eyes wide open, he was pouring out the coffee and uttering as he did so four words that became immortalised in our memories: "And now, the coffee!"

Had we imagined that long interlude? The conversation was resumed exactly as though there had been no interruption, and when the time came to leave we felt that, even if the coffee had been a little cold, our visit had passed without a hitch.

Before the new year the "eggshell" operation was completed and there were two new valves (which were absolutely superb – I know, for I spent all Christmas Day grinding them myself by hand). The whole thing was then closed up, to be out of sight, if not out of mind, until in Kano the engine was again opened and the crankshaft taken out for re-boring.

There was a never-to-be-forgotten dinner at the Lamberts' on New Year's Eve. I didn't know what to expect – a French festive family dinner was something new to me – except that I had espied a sumptuous chocolate layer cake being iced. For me the meal was a first in many ways, breaking records as the largest ever, as well as the longest, the heaviest, the richest, the oddest, the most gastronomic and the most diverse. There were snails, followed by oysters (flown from France), followed by succulent *entrecôtes*, all interspersed with other dishes too numerous to remember. The wines were superb. Of all the multitudinous courses none had been sweet, and yet the meal appeared to be finished. Amply fed though I was, I thought this was a strange lack – and – where was that marvellous cake? Well past midnight it was served as a meal in itself; oh so late, but I suppose better late than never!

Monsieur Lambert worked hard. Early and late he was out and about supervising the activities in the workshop area. And these Frenchmen did not merely supervise, they put on overalls and tackled the heaviest and dirtiest work themselves whenever necessary.

It obviously required lung power to keep the workforce on its toes. Round he would go bellowing as though the direst calamities were occurring on all sides. I picked up some of the words he shouted, but others were words I didn't know. I decided to ask Pete if he knew what the oft-repeated ones were.

"What does *merde, alors!* mean?" Pete fished around in his mind.

"Shit, well then," he attempted.

I had supposed it to mean something like "get a move on", or "not like that" – and I was more or less right, really.

A jeep arrived down the road that led from the north and pulled into the Lamberts' yard as we toiled there. Out stepped a young man who was bright yellow from head to toe. We were at first shocked, imagining him to be the victim of some fearful disease. However, his colour was caused by a coating of fine yellow dust found at a certain spot on the road. A few days later we ourselves turned a lurid yellow as the same dust settled on our skins on our northward passage.

Perhaps in the Sahara a little mint tea or a handful of sugar constituted riches. But in the lands we were passing through now solvency was money, money was a wad of grubby paper notes; and if there was none in your pocket, that was that. Only the hopelessly unprepared traveller came expecting banks in oases, offering traveller's cheques for petrol in the bush, and ending up a penniless parasite! Money changing did not have to take place in banks either but places such as the alleys of the Sabon-Gari quarter of Kano, where traders from far and wide assembled for this purpose.

Funds for our tour were lodged in the British bank in Nigeria, to be collected as required at certain points where there were branches. We now had to wait till we reached Bamenda for replenishment. But with so many unimaginable delays and such grand-scale expenditure on the car, even the large reserves we carried were running out. Before setting off again I got out fourteen UK pound notes, which I had tucked away, having intended them for emergency use in Europe. It seemed difficult to change them in Nkongsamba, but we talked to friends at the rest house and they put us in touch with an Englishman who was pleased to change the notes for us.

The next day, as we were preparing our departure, a member of the French community, whom we had met at the rest house, a quiet man named Monsieur Estrade, came to seek us out. He had apparently overheard the conversation of the previous day. Ignoring our protests, Monsieur Estrade pressed a large sum of money into our hands. He could not bear, he said, to think of two people travelling north without ample reserves of money. We could return it to him whenever we were again in French territory.

We were deeply touched at such extraordinary and spontaneous kindness and trust on the part of a complete stranger. An act like that shines in the memory like a bright light over the years.

Monsieur Estrade distinguished himself in one other way. He had once given me a lift in his car and is the only member of this French community who did so without trying to touch or molest me!

Chapter Nine

To Bamenda

People must not do things for fun. We are not here for fun. There is no reference to fun in any Act of Parliament.

A P Herbert, Uncommon Law

We were soon in the region of circular houses; the road was rough, the scenery marvellous. We spent the first night at Bafang in a coffee plantation. The maps bore little resemblance to the actual topography, but we arrived all the same in the highlands of Bamenda, a grassland region of exceptional beauty. It seemed light years removed from the coastal rain belt.

We had crossed into British territory. Even in this wild country there were reminders of the fact: knee-length shorts, driving on the left (if the road was wide enough to have a left) and mammy wagons, those ancient trucks overflowing with passengers (mammy wagons were forbidden by the French.)

It suddenly occurred to us to wash the car. We stopped at a river and gave it a bath – the first, and possibly the last, real wash and brush up it ever enjoyed with us – and it repaid our efforts by looking very respectable.

Then we ourselves had a wash; we brushed our hair and we polished our shoes. When we were all ready we made our "entrance".

Our first stop was at the doctor's to deliver an urgent package on behalf of a French government doctor. The doctor and his wife, both Hungarians, received us very cordially. It's nice, I thought, to be among English-speaking people and not have to make linguistic efforts, which was always rather a job for me.

"That's funny," exclaimed the doctor's wife as we were leaving, "your car is exactly the same as our forest officer's."

Feeling a momentary twinge of sympathy for the forest officer, we hurried on our way to the government rest house, a charming building on a hill high above the town of Bamenda. We were hungry and eager for the good dinner that we knew would be put in front of us there within the hour. Not to offend the sensibilities of my compatriots, we had to observe habits of dress, formal if not always comfortable, to which we had become unaccustomed during recent weeks. However, we felt well enough equipped with our new drip-dry "best" always at the ready for such occasions.

While I was changing for dinner a knock came on my door. Outside, outlined against the light stood a pinnate figure that seemed to flap like some mythical bird in a state of great agitation.

"I'm hungry, but I can't have any dinner. I've found my tie, but look, the cuffs – I've never worn the sleeves down before and they need cuff-links!"

I grasped the awful implications in a flash. I proffered a shirt of mine that was similar, but it was no good – though the cuffs were right, now the neck was wrong. There was only one hope – the marketplace.

Pete raced for the car, already put away in the garage. He turned on his heel.

"Wait," he called, a little addled and incoherent, "have we brought pounds, shillings and pence?"

"Yes," I reassured him. "But I don't think we'll need the pounds."

On the way down the hill Pete kept increasing the tension by remarking how hungry he was. I waited anxiously in the car while he combed the labyrinth of stalls. At last he emerged and his expression revealed that he now had the wherewithal to take his place at table with the best of us. As he got near he held up triumphantly a square of cardboard to which was attached a pair of large, tinny, decidedly tawdry tartan cufflinks.

"Didn't they have anything a bit more... er... conservative...?" I began.

"But they're the Cameron clan!" he protested; adding a moment later: "and they were only one-and-threepence!"

Our fellow-guests at the rest house, mostly couples, were a little aloof and uncommunicative. I imagine, however, that they loosened up when among themselves, especially now that the arrival of the strange couple in the car with French number plates provided a new topic for discussion.

Not quite extinct in these parts were remnants of a dying breed clinging to the true, traditional, white-man-in-the-tropics way of life. Inherent in this was a code of rules to be observed as rigidly as those of an enclosed monastic order. If one had to travel (heaven forbid!) one did so with drivers, a train of servants, bearers, and so on. The Bamenda community were upholders of anything they thought should be upheld. I think they were totally nonplussed to realise that in their midst was a manifestation of travelling-for-fun.

When, after a couple of days, we took ourselves off to roam in the marvellous area to the far north of the province, at night bedding down under the stars, no doubt the die-hard set thrashed out over their whiskies this mode of travel, a concept utterly alien to their way of thinking.

We spent a night among some pines, with an unforgettable dawn awakening to the muffled sound of drumbeats, a sound that always intrigued me. The sunrise was so beautiful that I tried to paint it. Pete made the breakfast, one of the rather rare occasions when I was let off kitchen duties.

The scenery of the region seemed to be more European than African; as Europe was in pre-history, perhaps, but embellished here and there with fantasies of nature. Any dwellings there were enhanced and never detracted from the landscape. There were lots of "mushrooms", anything from one- to three-feet high, sometimes covering an entire hillside. These eruptions were in reality dwellings of termites, which were always mushroom-shaped in this region. Elsewhere I saw them in the form of turreted fairy-tale castles, again quite surreal.

In the villages there were nomadic women called Bororos. They had very high foreheads and beautiful features, exquisitely graceful movement and long plaited hair. To my knowledge, I never saw any Bororo men; possibly they stayed in the mountains with their flocks while the women came to sell in the markets.

There was Wum, reputed to be a centre of cannibalism. I can't remember what it was like, as we passed very quickly through there.

The road curved back towards Bamenda. To the north there were no roads, a large area of mystery. All that was marked on the map was "steeply rising hills", words that caught our fancy, and we were almost tempted to round up some helpers, don our climbing boots and investigate. That feeling of being explorers must have got into our blood! However, we carried on towards the south.

We couldn't resist the strange land of Babanki-Tonga; that just had to be visited. Babanki-Tonga Land – uncharted and inaccessible by road – came into view in one breathtaking wide-angle glimpse. In the middle-distance from where we stood high in the hills, a cliff fell away, revealing a vast blue plateau on a lower plane. Not merely a plateau, it was like a chessboard, for spaced about on it were chessmen, as in a half-finished game. These were tall, narrow volcanic peaks. At the foot of one of these, though too distant to be visible to the naked eye, sprawled a village, Babanki-Tonga. We were in luck, because a ceremonial gun-dance was about to take place at Babanki-Tonga. We learnt this when we looked up some missionary friends of Pete's, the Schneiders. They themselves were going to spend a couple of days at the gun-dance festival and we were invited to visit them there.

Babanki-Tonga Land was further and even more extensive than it had looked from the road. Having driven to the nearest point, we left the car and started down a little path that seemed to be the obvious one to follow. But after a while, this veered away from the direction in which we should be heading, and we began to realise it was undoubtedly not the right path.

I tried to speed up my pace to make up for the time being lost. I was weighed down by a heavy bag of art materials, which I'd been unwise enough to bring, and I began to feel unusually tired. Pete had got ahead and, being on the wrong path, I couldn't dump my load to be picked up on the way back.

Then I came upon a little house standing in a fork where the path divided. Outside the door stood a man. I raised an imaginary gun, began to fire it and tried to do some kind

of dance. The spectacle seemed at first to daze the man, but pulling himself together, he showed me the right path to take. Ten minutes earlier, Pete had dazed him with a like performance.

At Babanki-Tonga village I could hear the guns, but found that the display was taking place quite a way further on in a woodland clearing. By the time I reached my goal, I felt thoroughly overtired; I couldn't even make much effort to appear normal, and the colourful spectacles I was so much looking forward to were lost on me. I just have some faint recollection of the men in gowns of great splendour and the women without gowns but with splendid ornaments.

So, when Mrs Schneider said she was going ahead to prepare refreshments, I was glad to accompany her to a little schoolhouse where they were camping. Inside I saw a camp bed, tottered to it and collapsed, incapable even of apologising. My hostess saw that I was all in, and she left me while she made a large pot of coffee, enough for five, three men and ourselves.

"Here's an advance cupful," she said. For me it was the elixir of life – I knew I needed more and yet more, unashamedly thrusting the empty cup forward, which I did repeatedly.

I had been extraordinarily tired and the coffee was extraordinarily reviving. So much so, that within a few minutes I was feeling almost normal again. Luckily a good supply of coffee was available and kind Mrs Schneider made replenishments following the demands I'd made on it.

After a meal (and more coffee!), I made light of the two-hour walk to the place where we had left the car. What's more, I thoroughly enjoyed the walk through a dreamlike landscape in the brilliant light of a full moon.

One should not underestimate the restorative powers that good coffee can have. But when I consider the effect that particular coffee had on someone as exhausted as I was that day, I see it as little short of miraculous.

We later visited the Schneiders and their colleagues at their marvellously situated Bamenda settlement, where they ran a hospital and a leper colony. One of their activities was to keep alive the very artistic native crafts of Bamenda tribesmen, woodcarving and work in bronze. Bamenda tables, round and often in the form of animals, are carved in one piece from a tree trunk. Primitive figures are made in wax and cast in bronze.

It was in this wild country that our tyre trouble began. I

remember stopping outside a village one evening when Pete had the task of taking off a tyre that had split. A crowd had collected quickly and were seating themselves behind us on a bank, in tiers forming an amphitheatre. They were engrossed in the action-packed drama, though there was no script, apart from some intermittent Dutch expletives! The finale came when Pete rolled away the useless tyre: the excited crowd sprang to their feet, the tyre gathered momentum and was borne away on a sea of arms, to start life again as soles to a dozen or more pairs of sandals.

The loss of two tyres triggered off a lot of trouble. We had the greatest difficulty in replacing tyres since the fifteen-inch wheel size of the Morris was smaller than normal for bush country, and this meant that we must pick up used tyres from any source we could find. While it was still fresh in our minds we added up the number of tyres we rolled away for sandals between Bamenda and Kano. It amounted to an incredible fourteen.

CHAPTER TEN

A grand finale

"What do you mean by that?" said the Caterpillar
sternly. "Explain yourself!"

Alice's Adventures in Wonderland

It was on a wild, dusty road near Bamenda that a chase took
place that can hardly have been paralleled since the days of
the Keystone Cops movies.

I had been painting and was wearing an old, paint-stained
sweater and a garment that was very original for that epoch:
a pair of ex-US army jeans, which I had bought in the Charing
Cross Road. As hippies and the like had not yet come on the
scene, I suppose I looked rather unusual and, apparently, a
bit tough.

As we rounded a bend, the figure of a man came into view,
seemingly lying in wait for us: and a short distance further along
the road a pick-up truck, a mirror image of ours, was pulled
up at the roadside. We were always glad to help in the event
of a breakdown, and if it was a case of a car like ours, then
the owner could expect immediate sympathetic attention. The
following conversation ensued, and I can report it word for
word, for I never forgot it.

"Are you in trouble?" asked Pete amiably.

Highwayman: "No. It is you who are in trouble."

Pete: "I don't understand."

Highwayman: "You slept in my forest."

Me (calling from the car, feeling indignant): "Kindly tell us who you are."

Highwayman: "I am the forest officer."

The forest officer, partially concealed behind large sunglasses, seemed uneasy, faltering in his prepared speech.

"No one can sleep in my forest. And anyway," he snarled, "you're not supposed to wander around the country like this."

That did it. Now quite ruffled, I jumped out of the car and confronted him. I drew myself up to my full height – five feet, eight and a half inches – and demanded elucidation. In response, the forest officer took to his heels.

I gave chase, but failed to catch up and the forest officer got to his car. He roared the engine into life and, without a backward glance, made off as though the devil himself were in pursuit. A reasonable enough person really, I didn't mean to look as menacing as all that.

"Englishmen do sometimes seem a bit scared of you," said Pete. "'I don't know why. However, on this occasion, I must confess you did look rather formidable!"

Suddenly we found that we were looking forward to the easy-going atmosphere that seemed to prevail on the French side of the border.

"They seem to like us there," observed Pete.

"You're quite right," I replied. "*Both* of us."

Before leaving Bamenda, there was one thing I'd planned to do: to visit the Public Works Department (PWD) and ask them if they'd be so good as to let me have a small, readily available thing needed for the car (I forget what it was – just

a screw or something). I told myself that, as a CDC official, I'd surely find a friendly reception, and probably a helping hand. But my polite request brought forth nothing – not the piece, no amorous advances, not even terror. All the PWD officer could rise to was a surly refusal.

Back at the rest house, I watched as Pete reversed the car into the driveway. Some government officials were hanging around, eyeing us with curiosity.

"Smokes a bit, doesn't she?" said a voice beside me as Pete revved up. Tactless to say the least! And then, as we made to get into our pick-up truck, obviously a two-seater, came the inevitable: "Where is your driver?"

After I'd turned and given what I hoped was a withering look, we made our exit. We didn't know that a grand finale was yet to come.

We were on the road heading east towards the French Cameroons. Ahead lay a British experimental tea plantation and beyond that the frontier. It was lunchtime.

Pete, who was driving, noted a small turning off to the left and made a snap decision.

"What an inviting little road! We'll explore it and then eat," he said as he turned into the track.

"We can't," I cried, pointing to a large notice that read: "ROAD CLOSED, BY ORDER, PWD." But Pete must have been in an impetuous mood, for he continued along the track for a few hundred yards, despite my protestation.

It was a sublime spot. We ate our picnic and had a walk before turning round and heading back to the main road.

"Quite honestly," I began, "I'm relieved we're getting back without incident onto the main road...."

My words were suddenly drowned by a dull rumbling towards our rear, which was accompanied by a curious shuddering like an earthquake, making the car seem to sway. The rumbling got louder.

We jumped out to look. We had just crossed a small bridge spanning the rocky bed of a dried-up stream. Though it *had been* a small bridge, all that remained of it now was a couple of planks, each about the width of a tyre. We could see the traces of our tyres; they had passed unwaveringly along the two planks with the precision of tightrope walkers. We could also see, through a cloud of dust not yet settled, a mass that had once been the bridge and was now just rubble filling the stream bed.

We drove on and out of the dust storm.

Earlier that day, outside the PWD office, I had remarked: "Come on. Let's shake the dust of these people off our heels." There was no way we could have done that more literally.

Chapter Eleven

The Three Musketeers

Friendship is constant in all things
Save in the office and affairs of love.

Shakespeare, Much Ado About Nothing

Kounden was a French Government research centre staffed by three young scientists, with whom Pete had established a firm friendship on his outward trip. Here we found a most enthusiastic welcome, a guest-room being thrown open for as long as we wished to stay.

Three bungalows clustered together housed our hosts, all bachelors, and in one of these we all joined for dinner on the night of our arrival. During the meal I tried to size up this engaging trio. Bernard, the director, was lean and fair, with an intelligent face; Roger was of athletic build, with good looks of a rather Mediterranean type; Jean was fair-haired, plumper than the others, and quiet but jolly. Lovely men, as the Irish would say. Any girl's heart would miss three beats in such company.

Pete and our hosts were obviously great friends. They asked what our plans were and pressed us to stay for as long as possible. We explained that we were already behind schedule, but said we would accept their invitation for a few days.

Later I had a game of ping-pong with Bernard. When the
game was over, Bernard crossed the room with a matter-of-
fact air, looked into my eyes and said in English, "Will you be
my lover?"

Roger, when he heard of my artistic proclivities, wanted to
have his portrait painted. So after lunch the following day, while
the others were escorting Pete on a tour of the centre, we
arranged Roger's living room as a studio, with an elevated model's
"throne" with a low stool on it for Roger to sit on.

He was a good model and the sitting progressed quickly. When the portrait was nearing completion, I turned the canvas round so that it faced Roger and I walked to his side. Together we studied the portrait. Then Roger rolled two very large and soulful eyes towards mine. The portrait temporarily forgotten, he told me of his great loneliness. While speaking he had been rising slowly from his stool and then he tried to steer – not only the conversation, but also me personally – towards the bedroom, the door of which stood ajar.

I laid my arms on Roger's shoulders, pressing gently downwards so that he sank again to the stool. He proceeded to speak further of his great solitude, a solitude that it was in my power to alleviate; tears seemed to be welling in his velvet-brown eyes as he again rose from the stool and resumed the steering movements.

This sequence continued for some time – rise, steer, sink, rise, steer, sink – until Roger finally came to the conclusion that there was no place for compassion in the British heart. He relapsed into deep thought for the remaining minutes it took to finish the painting.

In the forefront of our minds was a worrying fact that was by now becoming quite evident: the insatiable thirst of the car for oil was going to constitute a ruinous expense, not to mention inconvenience. Pete came back one day from a tour of the workshops. He seemed engrossed in thought, and from the enigmatic expression he wore, it was clear that some idea or other was brewing. "You know," he said at last, "there were several big drums containing motor oil. It's discarded oil that has been drained from government-owned cars. They do the oil change very frequently – quite unnecessarily so. There's gallons of it. Just think!"

I thought, as requested, and I quickly put two and two

together. I accompanied him to the workshops to examine the contents of the drums, and as far as one could see, it looked clean; it all came from these highly maintained vehicles – and it was there for the taking.

"There may even be gearbox oil mixed with it," protested our friends, who couldn't hide their alarm at our idea. But then they were, of course, under the impression that ours, like their own, was a serious car.

I tried to be level-headed in contemplating the tempting idea. These were comparatively early days, but the car had already shown its true colours; I knew it for the crazy car it was. Would it even get us to Kano? If it did, we could be beggared by the cost of oil by then. As for the desert, I secretly harboured grave doubts. Where were the limits of Pete's magical mechanical powers?

We reached a unanimous conclusion: any grubby old oil should be good enough. Indeed, anything better would be too good – pearls before swine.

Thus a large drum of – literally – priceless liquid was hoisted onto our conveyance, signalling an end to a nasty problem.

We spent some delightful days, going all together to see the sights of the region, a crater lake and another lake with hippos. The hippos preferred to keep their distance and eyed us from afar. I remembered them some years later when I witnessed the sad spectacle of a performing hippo in a Swiss circus.

Pete, Roger and I climbed the highest mountain in the territory, the Kougam. This was about the most arduous climb I've ever done: we started at dawn and got back about midnight. I made it to a shoulder within a few feet of the top, where one looked down the opposite side, a precipitous wall, and over a panorama of lesser hills stretching far across the frontier into the British

Cameroons. I should say "could look down", because it resembled nothing so much as my idea of the north face of the Eiger, and a quick glance was enough. What with vertigo, fatigue and the scorching sun, I thought that supine on the ground was the best all-round position just then.

"Leave the rucksacks here with me," I said, striking a magnanimous note reminiscent of some trusty Sherpa relinquishing all claim to personal glory. I must confess however, that for the last twenty feet of what I'd already climbed I had been both pushed from below and pulled from above.

The actual summit was a cone rising from the ridge on which I rested. It was not very high in itself or awfully steep, but it was covered with crumbling, slithering shale that, combined with the vertiginous aspect, made it very unattractive to me. Pete, good climber though he was, got to the summit slowly on all fours, admitting afterwards that it was unpleasant. Roger, who came from Narbonne, skipped up to the summit and down like a Pyrenean goat. On the top was a bottle containing half a dozen names and addresses. They had forgotten the pencil, which was in the bag left with me. Undaunted, Roger returned for it and was back on top within minutes.

Because the slippery summit was not my cup of tea, my name is not in that particular bottle. But it is in another, perfectly respectable bottle in a hollow tree at our lunch site, signifying an attainment I consider worthy of credit!

The next day our hosts were all very busy and Pete and I went to look up another young man living a short distance away, whose acquaintance Pete had made on his visit to Kounden a year earlier. I will call him Michel.

Michel was pleased to see us and we stayed to lunch.

Like most people living alone, he was a lively conversationalist. This was a period when attempts to introduce modern methods of agriculture and animal husbandry were meeting with resistance. Michel told us how a government department had had a prize pig flown from Europe for the purpose of improving the local stock. Exact instructions on feeding were given to the farmers, but these were not followed and in consequence the pig deteriorated. It got thinner and thinner and eventually was killed, for the pot.

Farmers were given implements and mules for use in cultivation, thus liberating women from the heavy work they were doing in the fields. The implements ended up as museum pieces on the wall of the chief's house and the harness was cut up to make sandals. The people preferred to cling to the old methods. "It's the custom of the country," they said. The International Labour Organisation in its field projects has done effective work in overcoming this resistance.

I already knew a little about Michel. When Pete first met him, he had had as mistress a beautiful girl of the Foumban tribe. Her name was Madeleine and she lived with him at his house. The story since that time was, I gathered, as follows.

One day Madeleine found she was pregnant. Michel was horrified and in a moment of panic evicted her from the house. Madeleine, at a loss to know what to do, went down to Nkongsamba to earn her living by working in a nightclub. When Michel heard this he regretted his action, brought her back to the neighbourhood and helped her to establish herself in a little house of her own. In due course the baby was born and it was now about three months old. According to our hosts, who had recounted these happenings to Pete, Michel did not believe that he was the father.

When we'd finished lunch, Michel asked if we would like to visit Madeleine whom, of course, Pete had met on his previous visit. We said we would.

On the drive to Madeleine's house, Michel assured us that he definitely was not the father of the child. "She had other men, you know," he said emphatically.

Madeleine came out to meet us when she heard the car. She was a lovely girl with a sweet, gentle manner. The house, which was tucked away in the middle of a wood, was quaint-looking, tiny and made of timber with a roof of reeds.

We went into the house and just inside the door was the cot. The baby was of mixed blood with rather European features.

Michel hastened towards the cot and forgot all the assertions he'd made on the way over. "Come to your papa," he cried as he picked the baby up to fondle it. He held it high in the air, every inch the proud father. "Handsome, isn't he?" he said to us.

Madeleine talked about her recent visit to the nearest town to register the birth. She showed us all the relevant papers and I noticed that the child had been given several names. The middle one was Colbert – Michel's surname!

We had coffee and after a while Michel whispered something in Pete's ear. It was: "Would you two like to go for a walk in the woods? I'll stay here with Madeleine. I want to give her a *coup*."

We had each heard this versatile French word used in many different ways, but we'd never before heard it used to refer to the act of love.

Jean and some of his friends were going on a flying visit to Douala to watch a football match, driving down one night and back the next. There was one free seat and, knowing that some things were needed from the Morris agent, he offered it to Pete.

Pete was ready to jump at the chance. When he told me about it, I reacted to the suggestion with some allusion to the hectic time in store for me, should I be left on my own at

Kounden. Pete, with a naiveté surprising in one with his recent inculcation, laughed the idea to scorn. "You mustn't class these men with the run-of-the-mill sort. They're highly educated, intellectual types. I know them well – they're close friends of mine and as such I know they wouldn't dream of making advances to you."

Then I enlightened him by telling him what I had hitherto thought best left unsaid – that two-thirds had already not only dreamed of making advances, but also got past the dreaming stage.

Pete didn't go to Douala. Jean found time in the few hours he was there not only to get the parts for the Morris but, incredibly, to buy some artist's materials I wanted. I was deeply grateful to Jean for such extreme helpfulness.

When the time came to leave Kounden, Pete said farewell to his three comrades in turn.

"Goodbye, my dear friends, Bernard and Roger; and you, Jean – the most tranquil of the three!"

Jean's reply came without a moment's hesitation. "Goodbye. You are mistaken, however. Not the most tranquil, just the wisest!"

I kissed them all goodbye and I felt a little pang in my heart as I drove away leaving my three handsome admirers standing in the road waving until they were lost from view.

Chapter Twelve

On the road to Ngaoundéré

Then a scream, shrill and high, rent the shuddering sky
And they knew that some danger was near;
The Beaver turned pale to the tip of its tail
And even the Butcher felt queer.

Lewis Carroll, The Hunting of the Snark

All we saw of Foumban was its fantastic carved wooden gateway.
We felt it necessary to cover ground and resist any temptation
to linger.

Banyo was perhaps the most picturesque town of them all.
In the central square were the most enchanting little houses,
whitewashed with very deep thatched roofs. I wanted to sketch
them. "Come along, there are plenty as nice further on." There
were, at the next town, Tibati, for instance, but they were not
the same. One should never let oneself be influenced by remarks
of this kind!

From Tibati to Ngaoundéré the road passed through wooded
country, the woods utterly unlike the rainforest. I was fascinated by all the unfamiliar and beautiful trees, as I had been
by the strange grasses of Bamenda. The baobabs, which grew
all over these regions, looked like children's drawings, slen-

der branches that didn't seem to match the huge, thick trunks from which they sprouted.

These particular woods were reputedly inhabited by big game. But the animals wandered at night only. If we drove with full headlights, countless pairs of eyes, large and small, were reflected. Many eyes in the upper branches glowed pink. Always it seemed inevitable that, as we drew near, slinking forms would be sighted; but no – never! Like a conjuring trick, they just weren't there after all. Since disembodied eyes meant animals, one could, I suppose, say I met some.

By day, when we stopped, monkeys joined us to provide entertainment that was mutual. They moved in packs and one massive, powerful member usually seemed to be asserting his authority. It was Grandpa who decided whether or not it was safe to settle down and study us and, if so, how near. Once I came face-to-face with an amiable warthog in a clearing. Otherwise, this wasn't at all the safari I'd been led to expect, it was more a case of Hamlet, not only without the prince, but also with scarcely any cast at all!

Our strangest experience of all was an extraordinary phenomenon that manifested itself when we were heading north and a few miles short of Ngaoundéré. It couldn't have been anything to do with wildlife – nor, seemingly, with anything at all. I could call it a "UCO", an unidentified crackling object.

It was a mystery on which even people long resident in the area were unable to throw any light.

We had driven off the road and found a good campsite for the night on level scrubland dotted with small trees. To the north lay flat country where, a few miles distant, was the small airfield of Ngaoundéré. We slept as usual up on the car, but without any awning.

In the middle of the night Pete woke me with a tap. I was quickly wide awake and aware of a distant sound to the south, which was growing in intensity. I jumped up and crouched. There was no moon and we made no light at all, yet I rightly guessed that Pete was poised beside me with a pistol at the ready. The sound was a crackling, as of a bonfire, and not only was it intensifying, but it gave the impression of heading straight for us. It was very frightening when it seemed it must soon be upon us. We never spoke while it raced towards us; when it arrived, it passed with a tremendous sound at a point about ten or twelve feet from the car, the spot where we had sat to eat our supper some hours earlier. It then continued northward at the same steady speed.

At no point had there been anything to see, no sound of hooves, not a breath of wind, only intense crackling.

After it had gone out of earshot, the crackling could be heard once again in the distance, about ten minutes later, now travelling from east to west until it finally disappeared.

When daylight came, all was normal – not a twig or leaf seemed disturbed.

What was it? More pertinently, what if we had been right in its path?

CHAPTER THIRTEEN

Poli – the little people

Everybody looked at Alice.

"I'm not a mile high," said Alice.

"You are," said the King.

"Nearly two miles high," added the Queen.

Alice's Adventures in Wonderland

Ngaoundéré was a beautiful town, as yet unspoiled by the ravages of progress. Very deep thatched roofs provided shade for the robed figures that drowsed during the heat of the day and a high thatched wall surrounded the palace of the lamido (king). I hope the lamido still reigns with the same pomp and pageantry, his sorties heralded by horsemen with trumpets three metres long. I saw crowds lining the route who shook clenched fists at his approach – quite alarming until someone explained that this is a normal gesture of welcome in Ngaoundéré.

The indifferent attitude to their responsibility of minor officials, those at customs posts, for example, was usually to our advantage; but not always.

It was necessary to stay in Ngaoundéré, as Pete was expecting an important letter. Every morning we hurried to the post office and every morning the young clerk shook his head after a cursory examination of the *poste restante* mail. On the eighth day of a "No – nothing" response, Pete became disbelieving and insisted that a search be made in case his letter had become misplaced, perhaps in an adjoining pigeon-hole; he even thought he could see a letter of the expected bulky aspect in one of the pigeon-holes, and requested to see it.

"Oh well," drawled the clerk, handing Pete the long-awaited letter. "You said '*poste restante*', not 'registered *poste restante*'." The letter had been there for nine days.

On leaving Ngaoundéré our target was Poli. Poli, several miles off the road, was approached through a valley lined with palm trees. Palms were reminders of the humid low-lying areas we aimed to avoid, but this was a tall, graceful mountain species.

There was a mission, where we stopped to deliver a quantity of mail and packages from another branch of their mission further south and, very untypically, were not even offered a glass of water by way of hospitality; and some miles further on we came to the village of Poli.

On the rocky hillside just above was a promontory on which stood an extraordinary rock in the shape of a colossal figure, keeping vigil, it seemed, over the village. I habitually seemed to see things in rock formations – monsters, houses, gargoyles, altars, fortresses, and so on. But this uncanny watchman, an Easter Island type of figure viewed from any angle, was the first thing to catch the attention – no one could miss him. We were not quite sure that he was natural – it seemed impossible – until we climbed up to investigate, and he apparently was. One felt certain too that the watchman must be revered in the village.

We took up residence under a large pom-pom tree (my name

– scarlet pom-poms dangled in profusion from the leafy branches)
close to the village, possibly a little too close to be entirely
tactful. At all events, our arrival did not create the usual noticeable
stir: on the contrary, there was no sign of life whatsoever from
the village. It was as though, sensing danger, the village had
withdrawn silently inside the protective cactus walls that
surrounded it. Only the stone watchman stood his ground. By
nightfall no one had come to call and there was still not a
sound anywhere, except, once, the cry of a black panther in
the hills.

"What about arranging an eerie blue light to shine from behind the stone watchman and observing the reaction of the villagers?" Pete said, grinning. "No one could be so cruel," I replied.

By the light of daybreak we noticed that numerous juju (voodoo) objects had been affixed to the trees and among the prickly cactus hedges, from which we gathered that our presence had caused alarm and suspicion. We were very sorry about this. While unsure of what kind of reception I'd get, I walked around outside the confines of the village in the hope of establishing friendly relations. I glanced hesitantly at the villagers, who were pretending not to notice me, perhaps on the principle that if you ignore something it will go away.

They were tiny people, the smallest I have ever seen. I was on a completely different scale, a being from another planet. Stooping somewhat, I offered some cigarettes and sweets to a group the other side of the wall and was pleased when they were accepted. The minute round houses were so small that a chicken perched in a doorway filled a large part of it. The houses were grouped in circles, eight or ten to a circle; only some were not houses, though they looked identical at first sight – they were depositories for grain or medicines with thatched roofs that tilted back like hinged lids.

In what I imagine might be called the main square, where a group of men were spinning cotton and weaving on a long loom, I could see the figure of a very old man, just skin and bones, lying in the shade of the biggest tree. He was probably a chief, or an ex-chief, and people seemed to be dancing attendance on him.

My friendly visit did the trick. In due course a small deputation approached our camp, at first with some diffidence. We offered various things in the way of gifts. The one thing our visitors wanted most was paraffin, of which we carried a good supply

for our primus stove. This was not wanted for burning, however, as I later saw it being used to massage Methuselah.

We had no lack of visitors after this – quite the reverse. A popular pastime developed. As we went about our chores or had our meals, we provided a continuous entertainment for an audience seated cross-legged on the grass. Our every movement fascinated and gave rise to much conjecture and animated discussion. It was a floating audience whose members came and went continually; "non-stop revue", you could call it!

Though this noisy audience was a trifle disconcerting, the show carried on for quite a long time each evening, just as we ourselves enjoyed wandering among the Poli-ites as they went about *their* business during the daytime.

And of course, now that their fears about us had proved

groundless, the strange juju objects were taken down from the trees and hedges.

Somewhere in the vicinity of Poli there was reputed to be a valley strewn with big bones. Years before, an outbreak of bush fire had caused a herd of elephants to stampede in panic in the direction of a cliff. Unable to halt at the cliff's edge, dozens of elephants fell to their death on the rocks below. I'm glad we didn't come across the place where something so horrid had happened.

❦

Garoua, a large port on the River Benué, was a relatively unattractive town. There were just two visits we planned to make in the region before pressing on.

Our first visit was to a Dutch mission, where, as had been reported to us on several occasions, vehicles using fifteen-inch tyres (the hard-to-find size we needed) were employed. So desperate was our tyre situation that we hoped the priests, if they had any tyres to spare, might be prevailed upon to sell. (A donation to the mission would be forthcoming and, hopefully, might help in securing a favourable decision!)

The priests were able to offer us tyres, but they were all far from new. We bought several, Pete resigning himself to the prospect of frequent tyre changing over the coming weeks as they gave out one by one.

Pete was interested to have an opportunity of chatting with his fellow-countrymen, and the priests were very pleasant. One of Father Paul's remarks, however, did not go down too well. At the time it was lost on me, as the men were conversing in Dutch when I joined them.

"So you're a journalist? How interesting!" exclaimed Father Paul. "And tell me, for which paper do you write?"

1 Houmsiki girl.
A painting in oils.

2 Houses and medicine
store, Poli.
A painting in gouache.

3 *Alamiya, Tamanrasset.*
   A painting in oils.

4 *Hoggar Mountains.*
A painting in gouache.

Paintings in gouache.
5 Tuareg goatskin tent.
6 Street in Agadès.

Paintings in gouache.
7 Entrance to Lamido's Palace, Ngaoundéré.
8 Peak Laperrine, Hoggar.

Pete named a national newspaper with a large circulation.

Father Paul looked crestfallen, but sympathetic. "Ah! Never mind, my dear boy," he said, giving Pete a consoling pat on the back, "we all have to earn our living somehow!"

Pete's face was a study!

The second visit scheduled was to a zoo that Garoua allegedly possessed. Having been so long in this particular environment without the hoped-for glimpses of animals (apart from the one obliging warthog), we both thought a visit to the zoo would be better than nothing. Unfortunately, we must have been given the wrong directions, for we never found it and, reluctant to retrace our footsteps, we decided to wait for the Algiers zoo.

CHAPTER FOURTEEN

To Houmsiki

...she could hear the rattle of the tea-cups as the March
hare and his friends shared their never-ending meal...

Alice's Adventures in Wonderland

We continued north into the Mandara Mountains.

The road wound over rolling boulder-strewn country that
might almost have been Cornwall or the windswept west of
Ireland, were it not for an occasional tall cactus. We knew we
were nearing Houmsiki when we saw on the skyline what looked
like cathedral spires; they were in fact volcanic peaks. It was
evening when we came to the brow of the hill above the village
and stopped to survey the scene; it took time to take in all
that lay before us.

This was just the second of several wonderful lunar landscapes
that lay on our route. I have a penchant for such landscapes,
never tiring of them and ever eager to paint them when I see
them. In fact, I see I'll have to resolve to limit my use of the
"lunar landscape" term!

We had just a brief, tantalising glimpse before darkness
descended. Below us the Lilliputian village was further dwarfed
by two extraordinary peaks that stood like sentinels on either

side; beyond, extending into the violet distance of the horizon, was a valley, looking very like the lower half of a cave studded with stalagmites.

The series of delays at the start of our journey had brought us to the season of the Hamatan, a West African wind that fills the atmosphere with particles of desert dust, impairing visibility. I knew of the effects of the Hamatan from the way the view of Fernando Po used to disappear for several weeks from my office window. We were very fortunate, however, in that almost all our time in the marvellous region of the North Cameroons coincided with a period of unusually clear atmosphere giving good visibility and wonderful colourings.

Government rest houses could be anything from the equivalent of a comfortable hotel to a bare refuge. Houmsiki offered the latter kind; it was very Spartan. One obtained the key from the village chief. But what the house lacked in comforts, it made up for in situation. Its verandah overlooked the entire spectacular valley. The possibilities for painting seemed limitless.

"I could happily linger here for weeks!" I exclaimed as I unpacked and spread my things around. To my dismay, Pete did not seem to be of like mind. Why? Carried away by enthusiasm, I'd overlooked two vital facts: first, our stock of meat was running low; and second, men set great store by such mundane things as full rations of meat. My heart sank when I thought of the long stretch of road that lay between us and Biu, the next shopping point. We'd need nearly all the tinned meat we had for that journey, which meant getting on the road very, very soon.

As fate would have it, I needn't have worried; a well-stocked larder, crammed with tins of meat and other undreamed-of delicacies, was at that very moment heading straight for Houmsiki and its rest house. This larder was an integral part of "Sweetie-pie"; "Sweetie-pie" being a large four-wheel drive Renault, a "Savannah", which was transporting its owner round the world and was now crossing Africa in the opposite direction to that in which we were travelling. Our respective paths, happily, converged at Houmsiki on that day.

"Hope I'm not intruding – I didn't expect to find anyone here." The voice belonged to one Keith, the owner of "Sweetie-pie", which had arrived noiselessly at the front of the house. We assured him that he was by no means intruding and very soon we were all great friends. Moreover, Keith was very public-spirited and took it for granted that the good things of his table should be shared. So it was that the three of us settled down to enjoy ourselves, and in fact, many of my memories of our long stay at Houmsiki are of sessions around the big table in the main room, the walls of which some artist had decorated with characteristic scenes of Houmsiki life. We enjoyed good food and good conversation, the latter consisting, of course, largely of travellers' tales. How we talked! On more than one occasion it was unnecessary for me to summon anyone to table for a meal; all were already in place, having sat on engrossed in talk ever since the previous meal!

Keith was an Australian. He was now on his third trip round the world. Travel had become a way of life with him – so much so that he just couldn't stop. He had tried; twice he had returned to his home town with the intention of settling down, but each time a few days of life there had been enough. He felt out of place in the house of the relations who put him up. It was impossible to do anything right; he kept using the wrong towels, forgetting to close windows and such domestic iniquities. "Sweetie-pie" couldn't conform to rules either; she brought mud onto the paving stones of the drive. She even fell foul of the police: the names inscribed on her sides, Timbuktu, Kano, and so on, were taken to be advertisements contravening legislation on the subject of advertising.

*

"Sweetie-pie"! One must be fond of one's vehicle, I thought, to give it a name. Certainly ours had none – anything appropriate would hardly be printable.

I wandered in the large village, which, like Poli, though far bigger, consisted of compounds ringed with protective cactus hedges or stone walls. Men wore gowns of cotton; women wore nothing except two bunches of large, light green leaves rather like lettuce. The bunches, worn fore and aft, were attached to a string tied at hip-level.

The village provided a riot of local colour. A group of men sat spinning cotton in the shade of an old gnarled tree. In one of the larger buildings women were busy making the apparel they wore for best; strings of dangling ornamental metal beads that replaced the "lettuce leaves". My attempts at conversation were useless and it seemed that most villagers knew no French, apart from one word, which they all knew very well – *cadeau*. (Pidgin English, in slightly differing forms, was spoken in the more developed regions of the French territory, but not here in the north.) I always envied Pete his remarkable gift for carrying on conversations, and seemingly getting messages across, where no common language existed.

I bought a little souvenir from an old man; it was a miniature brass jug, which he was wearing on a string around his neck, and through contact with his clothing it had become highly polished. I gathered that he used it as a container for snuff. We all liked the little snuff jug, so enquired where similar ones might be obtainable. They were made, we were told, at a forge in another village.

Pete and I decided to visit the forge and the next day, with a Houmsiki man as guide, we walked many miles across country to a very isolated village where European faces were obviously a nine-days' wonder. We were received by the chief, as usual a man of great presence and dignity; we bought some snuff jugs at the most primitive forge imaginable, and when we again climbed to the house of the chief to say goodbye, a gift was ready waiting for us – something that was undoubtedly of considerable value in that humble village – a handsome chicken.

During the walk back we passed an area where "lettuce leaves" grew in profusion. At this point our guide asked leave to make a small detour and Pete and I sat for a rest while he gathered a supply of "new clothes" to take to his wife.

We were uneasy about the future of our chicken. Killing and eating him would be unthinkable, and it would be most ungracious to offer our gift to the Houmsiki people. Hamish, as I christened him (though for all I know it should have been Hortense), had his own ideas about the problem, which was thereafter taken out of our hands. He saw no reason why a

well-behaved chicken shouldn't be a household pet and to support this contention he set about demonstrating absolute devotion. He refused to remain alone for a moment, following us from room to room and, incredibly, he didn't make messes indoors. We'd often wished for a pet and so far so good; but how would Hamish fare, we wondered, when we went on the road?

CHAPTER FIFTEEN

Houmsiki, Jos and Kano

"I'm afraid you've got a bad egg, Mr Jones."
"Oh no, my Lord, I assure you! Parts of it are excellent!"

Punch (1895)

There was one unusual day at the Houmsiki rest house. During the morning the two men appeared wreathed in smiles and swathed in aprons and altogether looking something like furniture removers in a farce. There was no moving to be done, and no furniture anyway, so I asked half-jokingly if they were thinking of cooking. Yes, they said, they were going to make a special omelette lunch and it was the cook's day off.

For much of the morning I was kept out of the kitchen, positively forbidden to enter it, while they applied themselves to omelette-making with the zeal of professional chefs in possession of culinary secrets that must be jealously guarded. Obviously, then, Houmsiki omelette was going to be exceptional and, hopefully, delicious – and indeed it was. How exceptional it actually was I learned later.

As hens were in evidence in the village, we had eagerly enquired whether we could buy eggs. It seems that in their desire not to disappoint, the villagers, having no new-laid eggs,

gave us eggs in the course of incubation. Pete and Keith discovered this after the special lunch had been announced and they decided to tackle the problem with a brace of teaspoons. That behind-the-scenes activity during the morning consisted mainly of laboriously separating the edible from the non-edible parts of all these "curate's" eggs; and as the non-edible constituted the major part of each egg, it was a very lengthy business. All of this was kept from me – wisely, for they knew that I couldn't otherwise have totally enjoyed my luncheon treat.

My reputation for fussiness was to my advantage in other instances, too. My two comrades were invariably anxious and willing to fetch water from the small well that was situated at some distance and served the entire community; it was a slow business. When the water arrived I filtered some for drinking and found it was so impure that the outside of the earthenware filter I used had to be scraped clean continually. It was not solely altruism that prompted the men to undertake the regular fetching of water. After we had left Houmsiki I was told the main reason: it was feared that if I saw the conditions at the muddy hole where it seeped slowly up from the spring, numbers of waiting feet immersed, I would refuse to use the water and insist on moving on, thus breaking up the happy party.

Houmsiki women were most attractive, especially the young ones with good figures and breasts that had not yet started to sag. "Pancakes", the men called the sagging kind of the older women. I thought "pancakes" were a result of going without any supporting garment, but the men suspected that "pancakes" were a widespread affliction normally disguised by bra-wearing.

I wanted to get one or two girls to sit for portraits, but was at a loss to know how to set about it. Even assuming I could make myself understood, which seemed doubtful, and the girls were willing, it was quite possible that their menfolk would object. "We'll see what we can do," said Pete and Keith, and off they went. They approached some senior village personages and, after much explanation concerning the requirements of art (*Non, pas pour baiser!*), they returned and reported success.

The same afternoon two beautiful girls arrived, covered all over with make-up and wearing the kind of ceremonial bead "garments" I had seen being made in the hut. The word spread and the idea of modelling caught on like wildfire. Before I had completed my first drawings, more girls started arriving on the verandah, where I worked. By mid-afternoon, the approaches to the rest house began to resemble a ceremonial procession. Most of the girls in the village, plump and slim, short and tall, most very attractive, had been coating their bodies with make-up and each was now longing to be chosen to pose. I was sorry I had to disappoint so many eager candidates.

I've always tended to coin words where no suitable ones exist, and I would have expected to be able to produce a name for anything. But there was an occasion at Houmsiki when I was stumped. Those barbaric bead "garments" that performed the same function as the everyday "lettuce leaves" (or the fig leaf in classical art) were very striking. Keith told me he would like to buy one to take to his girlfriend at home in Australia, but he was deterred from doing so because he didn't know what he'd call them when asked what they were.

It did constitute a problem and I thought hard for something to suggest. "Necklaces" had an anatomically wrong connotation. This was not the case with Pete's extraordinary coinage, but that was not repeatable. ("Shame-lip covers", Pete called them. This was derived from some Dutch pornographic term for female genitalia that could be literally translated as "the lips of shame".) I gave up. There seemed to be no easy solution; at any rate, none befitting the conversation of Melbourne drawing-rooms.

On one of my first days in Houmsiki, having explored the village, I started to walk up the road in search of a good overall view. It was in the full heat of the day and I had not gone far when I stopped, then hastened back down the hill again. A most objectionable smell had assaulted my nostrils. I'd been quick to realise what it was, for I remembered that the road over the hill skirted the cemetery, an area piled with stones. In Houmsiki, as in other rocky regions lacking soil, it was impossible to dig graves and the only alternative was to pile up stones to form tombs. Disliking the macabre, I dismissed the incident from my mind and never mentioned it.

One night I slept badly and was disturbed by nightmares. My bed was comfortable and I wasn't too hot, but I eventually woke in the middle of the night feeling like a rag. I got up and walked to the open door. A slight breeze was blowing from the direction of the village and the hill beyond, and it brought with it traces of the horrible smell, which I immediately identified.

At breakfast the next morning both Pete, who slept in the house, and Keith, who slept in a tent by his car, complained that they felt like rags, having slept unaccountably badly.

The wind changed and on the next and subsequent nights the prevailing fresh wind blew up from the valley and we all slept soundly.

We left Houmsiki, and at our feet in the car sat Hamish, never stirring until we were stopped. Then he invariably jumped out or in, as required. When we had to leave the car for any length of time we tethered him by the leg and he sat on his chosen perch right under the car, safely out of sight and in the shade. However, each time we did this the cord became wound round and round as a result of his continuous jumping on and off the perch, and we used to return to find Hamish lying helpless, one leg in the air ballet-style. This was not befitting our dignified pet at all. So we gave up tying him; we knew that a mutual trust had developed, and he was always there, hurrying dog-like to greet us.

But one sad day we returned to find Hamish gone. In one of the towns along the way we met some friendly missionaries who invited us to breakfast with them at their house in the country. On arrival there I could hardly say "Do you mind if I bring our pet chicken in to breakfast?" and so Hamish was left under the car in the back yard. "We'll watch him," called the boys from the kitchen. I had been too preoccupied with conversation to realise the need to tie him.

"He ran for bush," the cook informed us, too glibly.

Hamish was not in the bush and there was nothing to be gained by continued searching. A handsome chicken at large would naturally present a great temptation to the kitchen staff.

We continued towards Jos, slowly and unsurely, every few miles of progress bringing some new trouble with the car. Some were ills due to inexplicable causes. Whoever heard, for example, of the rotor in a distributor suddenly disintegrating? Yet I remember this happening, and Pete fashioning a new one Frankenstein-style, a collection of junk spread before him – some broken nuts, a wedge of timber, some glue, a file. The new rotor that was put together was not a monster at all; it was a real precision job.

We had become very sensitive and touchy about our car. We behaved rather like those parents who complain loud and long of the misdemeanours of their delinquent children, but are up in arms at once should an outsider presume to criticise. One day we were stationary at the roadside on account of tyre trouble when we heard the unusual sound of a car approaching. Who should it be but the United Africa Company's area manager from Port Harcourt travelling north in a large American limousine. He ordered the car to be stopped, got out and very kindly asked whether we needed help. Pete thanked him and assured him that it was only a question of changing a tyre and no assistance would be needed. The helpful well-wisher walked round our car and was surprised to see such worn tyres in use. Criticisms were well justified in the case of the two rear tyres – the ones that gave rise to the continual work, but on the front we had the two oversized tyres that we had bought originally, very tough tyres that we felt sure would see us through. They had never given trouble and were our pride and joy.

"The tread is a bit worn," said the man, peering into one of these tyres.

"Maybe," burst out Pete, with uncalled-for vehemence, "but the canvas is good!".

The journey to Jos was, by our standards, comparatively uneventful. The landscape of wild rolling hills was pleasant but monotonous. I had become blasé where scenic beauty was concerned.

Pete suffered from occasional bouts of fever, dating from a sojourn in the tropics some years earlier. His temperature rose to considerable heights, but he had come to take the situation in his stride, merely staying in bed when he felt it coming on and waiting for recovery, three to four days later.

Somewhere on the road after Bauchi Pete went down with this fever. I had witnessed one such attack while he was at Bota and thus knew from experience that patience was required. However, I felt uneasy alone in the middle of nowhere with a patient like a nuclear reactor on my hands.

Tired and looking forward to a little luxury, we arrived one night at the government rest house in Jos; it consisted of delightful individual bungalows with the comforts of a good hotel.

Ahead of us was a party of local officials and their wives who had come to join some friends; I was surprised to see the wives wearing, of all things, fur coats. It becomes quite cool in the late evening at Jos, cool enough for a fur coat to be just bearable but not attractive. An explanation dawned on me: the age of the status symbol had arrived.

We might have known that this rest house would be in great demand by those seeking a respite from coastal heat, and therefore was liable to be full. But when we arrived at the reception the news came as a disappointment. An Englishwoman, who smoked a cigarette of the kind that gets wedged somewhere in the mouth, greeted us with a perfunctory "full up". What alternative could she recommend? She suggested the Hotel Jubilee.

After some difficulty, we located this establishment, which seemed to be in a rather sleazy quarter of the town; I stayed in the car while Pete went in. Inside, his enquiries led to hopeless misunderstanding, eliciting the immediate summoning of the lovely seductive Miss Josephine, who emerged to lead him into temptation and the dimly-lit interior of the Jubilee.

I couldn't see what the place was like in the dim light. Best to go in myself and inspect it and hurry things along, I thought, when Pete didn't reappear at once. I was half-way through the door when I met Pete coming out with another man. Passing by, the onlooker had grasped the situation and wanted to assist.

"We can't discuss anything here," said the man, and turning to me, "it's no place for you to set foot in."

I hastily retracted my foot.

We repaired to the flat of some of his friends, members of the tin-mining community and, following my deliverance from the most notorious brothel in town, these nice people fixed us up for the night.

❦

For anyone crossing the desert by either of the two routes Kano was either a springboard or landing stage, in particular the Hotel de France at Kano. With cheap, simple rooms opening off a central courtyard, this was our billet while we had the car overhauled (some task!) and equipped ourselves with special requirements for our next stage – the desert. We needed a supply of spare parts, what and what not to take being an impossibly difficult choice. Here we needed powers of clairvoyance and short of towing a duplicate Morris behind, there was no easy answer.

The hotel was cosmopolitan. I sat in the restaurant and studied a cross-section of Kano society. At the next table an Arab trader, down from the north, gazed at his plate of meat-and-two-veg for a while before attacking it with his knife and fork in a remarkable fashion. Soon he gave up the unequal struggle and ate the whole thing with his fingers.

I thought the painted façades of the houses, for which Kano is noted, quite quaint and parts of the town were attractive, but in general it was at that time already robbed of some of its atmosphere by development and modernisation.

Here we came across none of the apparent disapproval shown by Bamenda types; we made many friends among people living locally. Robert, one of Pete's former friends, was particularly friendly and helpful. It was he who made us a present of our fine shovel for sand-digging, a tool as it turned out that was to be a lifesaver, in all sorts of ways. To us it was not a shovel, but a "shuffra", just as bottles tended to be "bottras", and so on. This was pidgin English, Loum variety.

The engine was duly overhauled and we got good tyres.

This was the point where most travellers in our shoes would have called it a day, and we must have seemed distinctly rash to head towards the desert, even with our car to some extent rejuvenated. Yet neither of us seriously entertained the idea of giving up. Kind Robert contrived to take me on one side to tell me earnestly of his opinion that the car was not quite fit for the desert. All I could reply was that I already knew that only too well, but that he was reckoning without a co-driver gifted with most extraordinary and unfailing wizardry in mechanical matters. Robert soon saw that no words from him or anyone else could shake my determination. "I think you're right," he said. "No matter what happens, he'll get it going again." Perhaps he was just trying to be kind; or perhaps he really believed it to be true, as I did.

No sooner was the car handed over for treatment than it was my turn to go down with a fever. The laundry couldn't keep pace with the demands I was making on it and I said to Pete, "I must have a new nightdress and you'll have to go and buy it for me. I want a nice one, especially as I like to look respectable if the doctor has to come!" He replied that he knew a good drapery store and off he went clutching a slip of paper inscribed with some vital statistics.

Lying there in the heat I looked forward to his return and the cool freshness of my new nightie.

"I hope you'll like it," said Pete as he handed me a remarkably small parcel. "I asked the man for a really good one and he recommended this – it's his top-selling line."

I don't know if it was the colour that did it, but the sight of my new nightie caused an immediate rise in my temperature. The nightdress (what little there was of it) was made of flame-red chiffon and the transparency of the material was just about total. It no doubt *was* a bestseller – among the girls of the Hotel Jubilee in Jos. This worsening of my fever was mercifully followed by a dramatically quick recovery, which I attributed to the horrific thought of having to receive the doctor wearing my new nightie.

When I was well again I took the curative garment back. The Lebanese shop-owner changed it for me, but he looked puzzled by my rejection of such a popular model.

It was getting late in the season to be heading north and desert-crossers arriving at the hotel were coming from, rather than going to, the desert. Those who came had crossed by the more westerly route, which is via Adrar, an artificial oasis called Bidon V and the great flat plain of the Tanezrouft ("Land of Thirst"). We got no first-hand reports of our mountain route, which seemed to be disapproved of. Ours was, I'm sure, the more exciting route, and we planned a thorough exploration of the Hoggar. This is more correctly called Ahaggar, but Hoggar is the name we always used. Very soon the Agadès-Tamanrasset section of the *piste* would be closed for the season; and if we didn't get going quickly, it might already be too late to join a convoy in the quite likely event of our being refused permission to go alone. There were even rumours that the *piste* was already closed. But we had long since learned not to heed any rumours. For example, we had been told more than once that the route by which we entered Nigeria just south of Houmsiki was impassable. In fact, it had been tarred, almost the only tarred road we came across in any rural area, and was the best-ever bit of road we encountered.

One night in the hotel discussion turned to a certain important festival held at a place north of Tamanrasset (the name escapes my memory). Throngs of desert Arabs assemble there once a year, coming from far and wide. Riotous feasting and merry-making continues throughout several days and nights. But not lovemaking. For, it is claimed, there is one very strange feature prevailing at this festival that inhibits indulging in sex. This is that any couple so bold as to flout this convention becomes inseparable – quite literally! Should this distressing situation arise, only the marabout (Muslim priest) himself is invested with the power to release the couple from their predicament.

Mass hypnotism, thought someone; something like the Indian rope trick. Nonsense, agreed others, don't believe a word of it.

"Wouldn't f... there all the same," came an English voice from the corner. "Who'd separate *us?*"

PART TWO

Chapter Sixteen

Zinder

"It would never do to say 'How d'ye do?' *now*," she said to herself: "we seem to have got beyond that, somehow!"

Through the Looking-Glass

It's April Fools' Day when we unfurl our Sahara maps and, noses pointing resolutely towards the Pole Star, set a northward course. After a few miles we cross the frontier into the territory of Niger and in no time are in the desert fringes, the savannah. We both feel an excitement that is mingled with a strange sense of unreality. Even the sea of thorn bushes to left and right of the road look unreal; the twigs are sprinkled with silver sand, creating an illusion of early morning frost on bare branches, ludicrously incongruous in the shimmering heat.

We reach Zinder, a small town and the last outpost of cement-built houses and full-scale French meals.

The car is going like a gazelle until, as we are entering the town, bang goes a shock absorber. Pete makes contact with – yes, they're back on the scene – some Frenchmen. He tells me that his new acquaintances are insistent on the advisability of having a spare car-spring with us in the desert. They are even prepared to forge one for us, and they urge the importance of waiting until the work can be completed. In fact, the work is put in hand before we have time to consider the question further.

The scene is a familiar one – some workshop area where the car is jacked up. It is about six o'clock in the evening. There are showers round at the back of the premises, to which I repair. While bathing, I hear sounds of a car arriving. This is undoubtedly the solicitous new friends; it has been mentioned that they are coming round with some refreshment. I immediately hear an imperious cry: "Où est l'Anglaise?" What unabashed eagerness to make my acquaintance! Again, "Où est l'Anglaise?" I hear nothing else.

After a while I emerge to find three very well turned out men pacing up and down like caged lions, as though suggesting I'm late for a vital appointment. One of them who has been scrutinising the bodywork of the Morris pauses, his hand resting on one of the wings; he looks at me and then says thoughtfully: "Oui, la carrosserie anglaise est vraiment très bonne." I'm not at all impressed by this impertinent stand-up comedian but, to be polite, I accept a glass of the whisky that is being passed round. It all has the unrealistic air of a scripted scene on a rather bizarre film set!

I seat myself on a low stool immediately behind Pete, who, with a mechanic, is crouched under the car. The stand-up comedian now seats himself on a box beside me. Accustomed as I already am to uncalled-for Gallic approaches, I'm not prepared for what follows. This man makes a grab at me and assails my clothing. It's as though the backs of the heads that peer under the car are movie cameras and we are two stars in a close-up for a shot – a daring "bodice-ripper" shot! Buttons and zip are assailed; my skirt is tugged so that I almost fall off the stool. Very reluctant to create any commotion, I strive to make a joke of it all while the tussle continues for some minutes.

I'm more than relieved when the examination of suspension mechanisms appears to be complete. The libidinous man, all ardour gone, is quite composed again.

It was hard to account for the outrageous behaviour. There must have been an ulterior plan that related to some kind of unilateral bargain they had in mind. They wanted no money for the spring they made for us. If this was indeed their game, how did they rate their chances of success?

Here I was in Zinder, in the so-called savannah, not the Sahara proper. I shuddered when I wondered what I might be in for in the central oases.

Chapter Seventeen

A hole in the radiator and trouble in a wheel

And certainly there *was* a most extraordinary noise going on within...

Alice's Adventures in Wonderland

The car trouble in Zinder marked the beginning of a new phase of crises, crises that were to become more and more sensational (unpleasant sensations at that) with remedies becoming more and more outlandish as time went by.

With us, seated on the back of the car, was a young South African, Dennis, to whom we had offered a lift (the blind presuming to lead the lame). Dennis was on his way to Scotland to join his fiancée. He had started out on his motorcycle, but near Kano had met with an accident that resulted in the motorcycle being burnt out.

The next crisis burst upon us somewhere on the road between Zinder and Agadès, when the radiator sprang a leak. After all we had experienced, I had come to regard most breakdowns with a certain stoicism; I'd become almost as immune to shock as I was to germs. If there were an exception, it would be a fault in the water-cooling system: anything like this I considered to be distinctly macabre.

An element of human error could have been involved in this (and perhaps also the subsequent) mishap. The road was rough and, apart from the addition of Dennis and his small amount of baggage, we were heavily laden. Pete was driving and, possibly carried away by enthusiasm at finding the car's performance much improved, he drove too fast for the conditions. It was not in character for him to do so, and it was on the tip of my tongue to say something, but I held back, always reluctant to criticise someone else's driving. It was presumably a sharp stone flying up that struck and pierced the radiator.

Dennis, grasping the nature of the trouble and possessing normal reactions, thanked us for the lift and said he would try to hitch-hike on to Agadès. "When I get there, there may be an Arab truck going to Tamanrasset that would take me," he said sensibly, as we moved off the road to set up house under a prickle tree. Dennis got his lift and Pete dismembered the forward end of the car and made an examination.

"Looks like we've had it this time." This depressing remark was one that Pete was wont to make at such moments and I had come to treat it with some reservation. It prefaced periods of deep contemplation, after which a plan of action would be put forward, considered and discussed. Then the chosen plan would be put into effect, usually despite awesome difficulties; and hours, or maybe days (and many Dutch expletives) later, we'd get on the road again.

"We'll have to seal off one-third of the radiator – there's no other way," was the pronouncement on this occasion when it came. I was asked to contemplate the entrails that coil to and fro behind the radiator grille and through which the water circulates for cooling. "Yes," I said, helpfully.

Out came the soldering iron to perform the delicate operation of linking two ends of piping, which in effect cut out the damaged portion of the labyrinthine watercourse. Exhaustive testing followed, during which at any rate there was no leaking. It was a big task and several days had elapsed when we finally continued on our journey towards the waterless wastes. Miraculously enough, the radiator seemed to function adequately in its impaired condition and continued to be watertight. We forgot our anxiety. We had already begun to feel that our car was some kind of super-cat, with ninety-nine lives.

We came to Tanout. There was nothing there but an establishment that served cold drinks; but what better could one want? I ordered a beer and Pete, a teetotaller, lemonade. As invariably happened, they were served the wrong way round. When I finally got my hands on that ice-cold beer, it was the most enjoyable I've ever drunk.

We were still some distance from Agadès when a very strange sound indeed was emitted from the direction of the front offside wheel. I thought at first it might be an ostrich (I'd seen some a few miles back), but later deduced that it was coming from the wheel itself. It was a long-drawn-out s-q-u-e-e-c-h, that is to say, a cross between a squeal and a crunch. It was repeated intermittently, sometimes several times in quick succession and then not any more, until a mile or two further on it would start again.

Under another prickle tree the wheel was taken apart and the source of the "squeech" located. I learned what a ball-bearing was like. A zigzag metal band that served to keep a collection of balls equidistant within the circle had broken up. Uncontrolled, the balls could orbit at random. Once in a while they all came together and this unhappy chance resulted in the sound.

A new problem faced us: should someone go to Agadès in search of a bearing of like dimensions, while the other stayed with the car to look after everything? We quickly agreed that there wasn't any choice open to us, so whether the bearing could survive or not, it went back into place and on we went, wincing at every "squeech" and the consequent mental picture of disintegrating metal balls.

Late in the evening, making the night hideous with sound, we "squeeched" our way into Agadès. Next morning Pete laboriously thumbed his way through tomes that listed spare parts for every manner of machine of French manufacture. It was a long time before he came across a roller bearing appurtenant to some moving part of a Citroën tractor, its dimensions corresponding exactly to those of the "squeecher". He wrote down the magic code number. A telephone call confirmed that the object was in stock in Zinder and within hours it was on its way to Agadès. The bearing fitted perfectly.

But the front offside wheel was not destined to live happily ever after!

Chapter Eighteen

Agadès

...Each formed a different view
(Long before the indictment was read),
And they all spoke at once, so that none of them knew
one word that the others had said.

The Hunting of the Snark

Agadès was fascinating. I hope it hasn't changed too much with
the passage of time.

When in contact with officialdom, one must always fall
into a definite category, and failure to do so may lead to
frightful complications. Strictly speaking, we fell under the
heading of tourists (even if the tour was utterly dissimilar
to any other ever packaged). Further, as tourism didn't really
exist in West Africa, we were in many respects a law unto
ourselves.

To put it mildly, I'm afraid our observance of formalities of
a purely bureaucratic kind sometimes fell short of perfection.
Nice as it is to feel that all documents are present and correct,
at the same time there is something to be said for a policy of
"leave-well-alone/bluff-your-way/muddle-through"; it's more
convenient on a journey such as ours was, and it obviates the

task of trying to see ahead. That's the line of argument we adopted, anyway.

I of course regarded planning to ensure safety and survival as vital, as did Pete. Other arrangements I generally left solely to Pete, with his first-hand knowledge of the regions concerned; moreover, a man positively enjoys organising documents, wrangling about trivia at frontier posts and the like.

Where the car was concerned, we lacked the so-called *carnet-de-passage*, a sort of passport for cars that was supposed to be obligatory. This particular bit of red tape was designed for a different kind of traveller, the conventional tourist who, with a time schedule, makes a plan. He starts out from home, where facilities are to hand to equip himself with all the bunches of papers he wants. So far, we'd never been impeded by lacking this document.

Where our passports were concerned, it was another matter. It was impossible to pass through the territory of Niger without visas – according to the book of rules. We had no visas, an omission that might have landed us in the soup. The direction of Pete's thinking in this matter was rather obscure, but he obviously decided on a fools-rush-in approach rather than risk refusal by the French authorities to grant visas. Indeed travelling for purposes of fun might well have been prohibited at that time in view of ever-worsening political troubles on some northern fringes of the Sahara. At all events, when the time came to present ourselves at the official rubber-stamping department in Agadès, we did so with passports that were deplorably unadorned by the necessary visas.

Dennis was again with us. His French being shaky, he was eager to accompany us to the commandant's office. There was nothing haphazard about Dennis's planning and he had taken care of all the preliminaries before leaving Cape Town. His passport, therefore, was the pink of perfection.

I overheard Pete chatting to someone at the hotel and asking the name of the head assistant at the office we were to report to. He described the appearance of the man he remembered and it was established that the individual in question was a Monsieur Blanc.

As we approached the office, three abreast, Monsieur Blanc himself, none other, was standing outside taking a breath of fresh air. He looked almost startled to see the impressive front bearing down on him.

"Monsieur Blanc, how are you!" called Pete with unusual gushiness. He waved his arm as he hurried forward, then brought his hand down to smack Monsieur Blanc in the centre of his back with a heartiness that startled him even further.

"Don't you remember me?" continued Pete without a pause, "and the time I was last in Agadès...?" And on he rambled, hardly pausing for breath. We all trooped into the office and were motioned to sit down by Monsieur Blanc, who was feeling quite knocked off his perch by having failed to recognise an old friend who remembered him so well.

Pete was ready with the three passports to hand over for stamping. Dennis's was on top. Mine was next. As a resident of Nigeria (of which the Cameroons was a part), I was entitled to three days in Niger without a visa. Pete's, which afforded no entitlements, was at the bottom. In other words, they were in descending order of merit.

Monsieur Blanc flicked open the top passport and was glad to see that everything was in order. Pete's he handed to a clerk so that previous records could be checked. Looking distinctly distracted by all the jabber, he reached for his rubber stamp and brought it down firmly on a page of Dennis's passport. Then, still trying to concentrate while the flow of talk continued, he examined my passport. He looked extremely uneasy and kept searching through it, but said nothing; in any case, it would have been difficult to get a word in edgeways. After much hesitation, he stamped it.

Now the clerk returned and Monsieur Blanc examined the third passport. He looked very unhappy as he pondered over his dilemma. We were a trio travelling together in one car and he could hardly split us up. The atmosphere was electric and Pete's chatter faltered. My eye fell on a wall calendar and I made a joke about it being Friday the thirteenth, which seemed quite uproarious to Pete and Dennis. After a long delay Monsieur Blanc stamped the third passport.

Pete continued to keep up a strange, inconsequential chatter throughout the remainder of the proceedings.

The passports finally had to be presented to the chief for signature, and at that moment a figure looking eight feet tall loomed in the doorway like the menacing black cloud that heralds a sandstorm. The chief himself walked in. He was a saturnine man with beetling brows that beetled even more when he looked at us. Even Pete's vocal flood dried up whenever he did this, which was frequently so that the chatter came by fits and starts like a wireless set in a state of oscillation. The man kept studying the passports as though they contained lengthy and absorbing reading matter while Monsieur Blanc kept on and on trying to hand him a pen.

The chief looked daggers at Monsieur Blanc, but his policy was clearly not to let his assistant down, and he signed the three passports. By this time Pete and I were little more than nervous wrecks, a condition that to some degree seemed to have communicated itself to Dennis.

We left Monsieur Blanc outside his office having a little more fresh air and hurried away into the sunlight.

Agadès was a town constructed of golden-yellow mud. I watched a plasterer at work: his plaster was mud with an admixture of grass as coherent. No cement or new-fangled tools for him; his left hand served as a hod and his right hand as a trowel. I thoroughly approved of this method, which was not very unlike my own unsophisticated method when I had plastered my mother's summer cottage in Ireland some years previously.

Facing the hotel across the main square was the mosque, with its slightly surreal tower tapering skyward. This tower was the most characteristic thing of Agadès. It was like a stickleback; wooden beams incorporated in the structure protruded all over. "Those beams are rotten. I wouldn't go up if I were you," people said, and it did look rather a flimsy sandcastle.

But one day when I found the door open I went in and crept up the spiral mud staircase, for which I seemed to be too large — I almost didn't fit at all! I squeezed my way to the top. I was not going to call the faithful to prayer, but to look at the view over the town. Emerging onto the small space on top, I didn't after all stay long because, although it was open to the sky, I was overpowered by a sickly sweet scent that pervaded the mud floor and parapet.

Down again in the square, I was delighted to see an open truck drawn up that provided an ideally elevated platform from which to sketch. I raced for my drawing-board and climbed up, getting just the viewpoint I needed to paint the mosque.

Later on Pete drove back from a visit to his Arab friends. I got into the passenger seat. Phew! Scent! "What on earth…!" I began, and then stopped to think. I refrained from accusing him of having a woman in the car when I remembered the perfume on the tower. It was actually Si Kassim, the marabout, who'd been taken for a drive and had left cloying traces emanating within the car.

Si Kassim invited us to coffee at his house and we joined the all-male circle already seated round the floor. The Arabs could never disguise their last-come-last-served attitude towards women, but I tried not to think too harshly of them, for it was really a great honour for me to be invited at all. Fine people, the Tuareg, I thought all the same, with their matriarchal society!

Tuareg, those wild and magnificent nomads, abounded in Agadès. Men were veiled right up to their flashing eyes. Unveiled Tuareg faces, of boys not yet veiled and women, were often beautiful. They had a delicate cast of feature and skins that would be light were it not for the dye that rubbed off the indigo cloth in which they were swathed. They were said to encourage this, as the dye was alleged to protect the skin from the sun. They may have been right; they had many herbal remedies that seemed to be effective against the ailments that afflicted them. They even had no need of the contraceptive pill, so I was told, for they had an equivalent, a secret known only to Tuareg women.

Abdul Ahmed had not been forgotten and his little package was duly delivered, enabling Abdul – as broken down as ever – to put to the test the long-awaited aphrodisiac remedy. Then followed a period of suspense when much of Agadès (Abdul had numerous relatives as well as wives) waited for news. Hope springs eternal and I understood that the prevailing mood was one of optimism. We ourselves did not pin great hopes on success in Abdul's case. The root of the trouble was more likely to be advancing years rather than any physiological impediment that might have responded favourably.

It was several days before the verdict reached us. I would like to be able to report otherwise, but alas, to everyone's great disappointment, the yohimbine had no effect.

Nevertheless, Abdul was very happy to have had the

opportunity to try this last resort, failure though it was. To express his gratitude, he lent us one of his houses currently unoccupied. It was cool and pleasant and consisted of a couple of large front rooms, a central area open to the sky, and the women's quarters beyond, well cut off from the outside world. The latrine was a shaft bored to great depth and seemed to be hygienic and odourless. This house made an amusing change from the hotel and we stayed there for several days.

One of my memories of the Agadès hotel is of being awakened at dead of night by the sound of men's voices singing, presumably on the roof above me. It was so loud that there was no question of trying to sleep through it, so I just lay awake and listened. The odd thing was that it was not like the singing one might expect men to indulge in late at night on a hotel roof. Whether it was a regiment that hailed from somewhere where good singing is endemic, as in Wales, or whether it was some kind of improbable Saharan choral society having a two a.m. practice, I can't speculate! But it was excellent singing and for some years I could remember the bars of a rousing marching song, though I've never heard it before or since.

We visited the military control (not Monsieur Blanc's department!) to announce our intended departure for Tamanrasset. Not without trepidation, for a refusal, or insistence that we could go only in convoy on this, the most difficult and dangerous section of the *piste*, seemed quite on the cards. But to our relief we got authorisation to go alone, after they were satisfied that we were aware of water and petrol requirements and correct procedures. No deposit against the cost of searching if we became lost was demanded (how rash!), but they did try to hustle us on our way. We wanted to be allowed as long as possible on the route, but the most we could stretch it to was five days to get to In Guezzam, the oasis roughly half-way to Tamanrasset.

Closure of the *piste* was imminent. Two men left a couple of days before us in a Land Rover – two hares in comparison with two tortoises – and their tracks were helpful to us for a day or so. After our departure one Arab truck would be leaving, then nothing more. We were glad to know that the truck would be coming after us. We planned to make as much headway as possible early, because after being overtaken we would continue in the chilling knowledge that we were the last on the *piste* for the season.

Dennis, it need hardly be mentioned, elected to go on the truck with the Arabs.

CHAPTER NINETEEN

Agadès to In Guezzam

"...And the moral of that is – 'The more there is of mine, the less there is of yours.'"

Alice's Adventures in Wonderland

One afternoon, at the hour when the heat begins to diminish, Pete and I climbed into the car and set off, as we had done many times before. But this time it was a special departure – we were launching into the desert proper and onto the *piste* proper.

The *piste* was well defined by means of tall posts so placed that from each post the next one was visible; sometimes it was necessary to stop and scan the horizon at length, but eventually one should always be able to spot it, even if just the top.

Following Arab custom, we rested during the heat and drove in the cool part of the day and at night. After dark, of course, it was dangerous if the *piste* was not clearly discernible – often for many miles there was nothing to go by but the posts. Once (and once only) we inadvertently wandered from the road and were lost. Back on our tracks we hurried until we saw posts once more. At one point I noticed a crossbar on a post. This had been erected as a memorial to the party with the Morris Minor at the point nearest to the disaster site.

Much of the *piste* was corrugated, an effect of the wind, and rattled our teeth almost out of our heads. There being only two ways to drive on these corrugations – very fast or very slow – we had no choice; for us it meant very slow. We didn't complain, though unpleasant as the washboard was, it at least confirmed that we were indeed on the *piste.*

Often we came to patches of deep, soft sand known to Saharans by the Arab's word for it, *fesch-fesch. Fesch-fesch* was piled like snowdrifts, and it was in this that our car lacked the necessary power to keep it moving. If once we came to a standstill it could mean a lot of toil and sweat with the shovel before we could get on our way again. Sometimes when we became stuck in *fesch-fesch* for the umpteenth time late in the evening, it was the last straw and we would just leave the work to be tackled first thing in the morning; then we'd settle down for the night, sleeping behind the car in the middle of the road, where the ridges of soft sand constituted a most comfortable bed. Our airbeds had long since come to grief under the thorn trees of Agadès.

We seldom suffered from heat as long as we kept to the essential rule of resting in the heat of the day; not to do so would be madness. The degree of humidity in the desert air being so low allowed sweat from the body to evaporate instantly. Thus one feels comfortable, with none of the accumulation of sweat on the skin that makes you long for a shower. The Tuareg, although they seldom wash in water, give no impression of being dirty or unhygienic. This is quite natural because, without accumulations of sweat on the body, odours apparently just don't form.

The nights, mornings and evenings seemed marvellously cool. The sky at night was quite magical. When driving, our headlights seemed to bore a bright golden tunnel of light through surrounding darkness that was blacker-than-black in that unpolluted air, and somehow seemingly solid like an archway of trees. I don't quite know why, but it never failed to remind me of driving at night, with headlights, along dark tree-lined avenues that led to old Irish houses. That had given the same "tunnel" impressions.

In total darkness, the stars were a wonderful sight. Dominant in the southern sky was the Cross of Agadès, a constellation used for navigation by the Tuareg and also as their symbol on swords and on the front of camel saddles. Like others before me, I'd thought it might be the Southern Cross, but that is nearer the horizon and much less significant viewed at that latitude.

While in Agadès I'd spotted a silver cross of Agadès being  worn by an old man, the sort probably forged from old coins. I succeeded in buying it from him, and it is one of the few mementoes I brought back with me.

Before going to bed at night I made a practice of erecting a screen over my head as a shield from the moonlight, which in that atmosphere shone with an intensity that was disturbing and almost uncanny. My "moon defences", as I called them, were essential and, except on totally moonless nights, I couldn't sleep without them.

In Abangarrit was the name of a large circular well, providing the last fill-up of water until In Guezzam, 132 miles distant. It was water of beautiful quality, but I noticed it had an odd, grassy, slightly farmyard smell (Pete didn't notice it). Could it be linked to camels?

The *piste* led slightly uphill as we left In Abangarrit. The terrain was mostly rock and stone, but the *piste* itself was piled with soft sand in patches. At times we came to a standstill, we dug, we pushed, the engine roared, the wheels spun, to no effect.

"A tin of fruit," I said, knowing that things had gone on long enough to make it a "tin-of-fruit" occasion.

We sat down ceremoniously and Pete operated the tin opener while I got out two bowls.

The moments that followed provided an insight into the effects that life in the desert can have on the thought processes. The tin contained eleven peaches. Pete counted and then re-counted them. He assessed their comparative sizes, chose one and with great precision cut it in two; then he put five and a half peaches in each bowl. The Crown Jewels could not have been treated with greater deference.

"Do you agree that that's an even division?" he enquired in judicial tones.

While driving the next morning we came upon a Tuareg camp, a huddle of tents made of goatskin. A group of girls ran to meet us in a state of high excitement. I was the main centre of interest and faces crowded into my window. I had on a sun-top of stretch towelling, which was swathed under the armpits and held in place when tucked over the top of a strapless bra. This incomprehensible arrangement aroused unrestrained curiosity. The girls put their arms through the window and tweaked at my apparel, while the bra itself and how it came to be self-supporting were obviously matters of infinite wonderment. Always, I found Tuareg women to be intrigued by my clothing.

Early one evening the roar of the Arab truck that had left Agadès after we did could be heard. This, and the brilliance of the headlights as it crested hill after hill, suggested that it would reach us very soon. In point of fact, it was still several hours' journey away. Time and time again it would sink from view into a hollow, only to roar into view again later on. Every so often I'd exclaim: "It's almost here, it must be time to run to the road to meet it." But Pete knew better from experience. "It'll be more than an hour yet." At about midnight it really was close. It stopped, as all who pass one another in the desert do. Dennis got down from it and chatted to me while Pete talked to the Arabs. I warmly congratulated Dennis on having found a safe and sure means of transport! After a few minutes they wished us luck and rumbled away into the night.

Now that they were gone, the *piste* would be deserted until winter came again, and this knowledge lent an air of even greater desolation to the desert.

At one time the name Sahara might have suggested to me an expanse of sand, totally flat, and little else except, perhaps, a disagreeable sensation of agoraphobia. Our Sahara route was not like that. On the contrary, the scene was a frequently changing one filled with incident and contrast. Not more than a quarter of the whole area of the Sahara is covered by sand; the sandy zones ("ergs") have dunes that can reach heights of 600 feet. A "reg" is a flat, stony plain with outbreaks of rock; for the rest, there are plateaux and mountain ranges.

One morning did find us on a stretch of conventional agoraphobic desert terrain. It was as flat as a billiard table. Only a range of deep blue mountains to the west relieved the unpleasant monotony of the landscape, but they were in fact very far away.

It was in the middle of this plain that something gave way, emitting a sound like a sigh as it did so. At the same time, the car collapsed at one corner – the front offside.

Then followed the usual routine – examination, profound thought regarding diagnosis of problem and possible solutions.

On this occasion I didn't interrupt the important thought processes and carried on with the household chores, exercising stringent restraint in the use of water. As regards washing, this is easy; as there is no dirt in the air or on the ground the sand is clean and pure and one can adopt the Tuareg method of "washing" one's hands in sand. I invariably did the washing-up in sand, which was actually far better than water for the purpose. Pete was just pottering about and rummaging in all kinds of things.

Quite late in the evening there were signs of activity. Many tools were laid out; I saw a metal saw, a wood saw, a measuring tape. Work went on by lamplight. When no more help was wanted I went to sleep.

At first light I opened my eyes. All was quiet and Pete was asleep. I looked at the car and saw that it had risen to its normal position.

I'm not familiar enough with all the mechanisms in the lower regions of cars to recount just what had taken place. I know only that some metal support rod (not a torsion bar) had been replaced overnight, and that also our smart shovel, which had had a long wooden handle, now had a noticeably shorter one. Where Pete was involved, there seemed to be no lengths to which improvisation could not be stretched. This breakdown could not have occurred at a worse time and it had been crucial that we keep going as scheduled. It was my confidence in Pete's skills that had enabled me to take in my stride all the stresses and strains. The way we drove off that morning and continued north seemed to prove yet once more that my confidence was justified.

We spotted a miniature thorn tree close to the road. It provided a modicum of shade and we pulled in under it for lunch and a siesta. Suddenly, as we rested on the sand, three or four tiny birds appeared from nowhere. How they came to be under the tiny tree, so far from oasis or waterhole, struck us as very odd. Odder still was their behaviour. They insisted on getting inside our shirts and nestling close to our bodies. They were completely trusting, and bore with us patiently when we had to disturb them temporarily to move. When the heat had passed and it was time to drive on, we didn't attempt to take the birds with us but perhaps childishly we left a bowl of water in the shade of the tree.

Tuareg mixing bowl

CHAPTER TWENTY

In Guezzam to Tamanrasset

At any other time, Alice would have felt surprised at this, but she was far too much excited to be surprised at anything now.

Through the Looking-Glass

One entered In Guezzam through an archway. Inside was a square courtyard, in the centre of which was a well. Surrounding the yard was a low building incorporating a few rooms for travellers. There was a petrol pump issuing fuel at a very elevated price, and there was a radio station manned by two bearded Frenchmen – the sole occupants of the place. That's all.

In the evening the pastimes were card games or boule – that very popular French version of bowls. I volunteered to play boule with the bearded pair. As the contest got under way I played very well – I was even starting to beat my opponents. This was something that could not be tolerated – I was not well versed in these special rules of etiquette – and thereafter I noticed that, with a baseness that could not be expected of these upright, honest gentlemen, they started to "manipulate" the scoring, imagining that I wasn't paying attention to it!

More time was spent in talk than in anything else: talk and jokes that were as continuous and rugged and rude as the mountains. While they were guarded when I was present, the gist of their bawdier chatter sometimes reached my ears all the same. Tall stories abounded, usually revolving on sexual exploits on leave in Algiers, or at some outpost where female wayfarers (who seemed always remarkably compliant) came along.

Our bearded friends, who had the task of monitoring our journey on the next and perhaps most difficult stage – the hop to Tamanrasset – accorded us plenty of time for loitering en route.

We loitered first – intentionally, this time – among the rocks that rise from the sands some thirty miles north of In Guezzam. We used as our house a cave, like an igloo inside, round and cool with a couple of natural windows for light and good ventilation; they gave on to a spectacular view, for good measure. I'm sure we cannot have been the first tenants of this cave; it could even be one of the oldest dwellings on earth. All around was shimmering, rippled sand, out of which high gold and purple rocks billowed up, in form like the supra-mundane mushrooms created by atom-bomb explosions. The smooth stem-like bases had been heavily eroded by driving sand, and each outcrop stood in the centre of a sunken basin formation in the sand, as a seashore stone rests in a hollow made by the swirling tide.

I thoroughly enjoyed the few days of Neanderthal life in my cave!

One night we were having our meal by the light of a hurricane lantern. Beyond the small pool of light it cast, the night was as black as pitch, the moon having not yet risen.

Without any warning the silence was shattered by a sound

alarming in its unexpectedness – a thunderous roar not fifty yards away. To me a roar suggested a lion; the lion was once king of the desert, but that was in very ancient times. I was quite nonplussed and Pete, normally talkative, said nothing.

I had begun to think my ears were deceiving me when, with the soundlessness of an apparition, an austere figure emerged from the blackness to take shadowy form on the perimeter of the circle of light. We raised the lantern to extend its range and there stood a Tuareg man, his arms outstretched in front of him, holding with both hands a goatskin bag. There was clearly a smile in his eyes, just visible above his veil. We beckoned the stranger to join us and he advanced slowly and seated himself cross-legged on the ground facing us.

The roar we heard was emitted by his camel when it was made to sit down; later on I noticed this to be a camel habit.

As far as we could make out, the Tuareg was all alone and was heading for the south-west. He had just milked the camel in order to bring us a present, and the milk when he poured it out for us was still hot; it tasted strongly, too, of the rancid butter used to treat the goatskin to keep it supple.

While I looked out some of the ever-prized sugar and green tea, Pete embarked on one of the remarkable conversations that he conducted when there was no common language. This one consisted mainly of naming places to which the Tuareg might possibly be going, or might know, in the French Sudan. The mention of a recognised name elicited a delighted response, the name being repeated and savoured at length.

The portions of tea and sugar that I wrapped in paper were accepted with alacrity. Each of these our visitor poured with dexterity into folds in his garment, which he then knotted tightly to form several tiny bundles in the cloth.

He had the usual Tuareg air of graciousness and dignity; this is not confined to noblemen, though he may have been one. In a short while he rose to his feet and took his leave of us, an evanescent figure that retreated and vanished as silently as it had come.

❧

We braced ourselves for the next fifty miles, which were marked "*très difficile*" on the map. They didn't seem to us any worse, however, than the rest.

As the *piste* became a rocky track in the foothills of the Hoggar Mountains, we made great headway. Up hill and down dale, we forged ahead, right to the town at the heart of the Hoggar, Tamanrasset. Not surprisingly, we'd kept up quite a pace: we had faulty brakes.

The car troubles that had dogged us ever since the start of our journey were now to excel themselves in the final and most ludicrous phase of all. They reached their zenith during the weeks we spent at Tamanrasset. The crazy situations we had already survived were as nothing compared with what was to come. From bizarre to berserk, from far-fetched to farcical, the calamities befell us thick and fast.

Our first task in the red-mud town of Tamanrasset was to send a cable to Algiers for (among other things) whatever it was that was needed for the repair of the brakes.

A trip to the tailor and the shoemaker came next. To be sartorially correct meant a *serwal*, which was a pair of loose black cotton pants with elasticised waist and ankle; it was cool, comfortable and was the most modest of garments for sitting cross-legged on the ground. A special belt of leather thongs was slotted through at the waist. It was also necessary to buy Saharan sandals, which are as large as plates and, unlike normal sandals, do not shovel up sand under the soles of the feet. This outfit was worn by all – men, women, children – even the military. (The French can be very sensible; it is difficult to imagine the British Tommy in *serwals* and open sandals!)

Chapter Twenty-one

Taza

I have heard whispers, have seen shadows moving
On the mountain of Taza, where men fear to tread.
By the moon's cold light I have heard voices calling –
Is Taza then haunted by shades of the dead?

In days that are past there were brigands on Taza;
They went forth from the mountain to pillage and slay,
When the camel trains laden approached through the
      desert
They were guided by voices to seek out their prey.

From the tomb voices spoke to the wise ones of Taza,
To the elders who listened, ears pressed to the graves.
Were these then the echoes I heard in the moonlight?
Do the shades of the brigands still lurk in their caves?

Rosamond Willes, "The Voices of Taza", inspired by
stories and paintings of Mount Taza in the Hoggar
Mountains

We hoped the part for the brakes would come quickly (in fact it took weeks). In the meantime excursions by camel seemed the obvious thing; although camel-riding is considered to be uncomfortable and apt to cause seasickness, I found it not too unpleasant.

Pete wanted to visit Taza, which he had never seen, and as he had often mentioned the spooky mountain I was keen on visiting it too. I asked some of our Tamanrasset friends about it. They seemed reticent on the subject; none had ever been there themselves, but they did hint that there was something sinister about the place. The only odd fact that emerged from my enquiries was that Taza was a place shunned by Arab and Tuareg alike; none would go anywhere near it.

Pete had heard of a camel owner who was willing to escort people on expeditions they wished to make by camel. "Will you please hire us camels and take us to Taza?" we asked the man, through an interpreter. Back came an emphatic reply on the lines of "not on your life!"

"He says his brother took a party there last year," said our interpreter, "and the poor man has been out of his mind ever since. They say the mountain is haunted and you might as well give up the idea. No one will take you there."

That served to cement our determination. Repellent to others, Taza became magnetic to us. Pete thought we should drive there, though that seemed the very last means to try. Brake trouble apart, there was no road. "Out of the question," said anyone we talked to.

Off we went, following a winding *oued* (dry riverbed). It was a ribbon of rough boulders, pebbles and sand that wound through mountainous country. People thought that this drive would tax the powers of any vehicle: the Morris handled it perfectly. Without a murmur of complaint it crept along, delivering us right at the foot of the mountain we were heading for. Good brakes were not a priority in the *oued*.

In front of us where we came to a halt was a small stone-built dwelling, once the house of a hermit. Inside the doorway of the little house we found large sacks, which the last occupant had abandoned. They were full of rice, sugar and other commodities, and the fact that they were completely intact and undisturbed testified to the fact that Taza, despite having a year-round supply of excellent water, was not visited by nomads or travellers. We found the well a few yards further on; it was surrounded by green vegetation, in a charming spot.

Taza was in the shape of a table mountain, or rather a table hill; everything was on a small scale and you could scramble all over it in a couple of hours or so. Deserted hermits' houses peppered the slopes; it looked as though at times there might have been quite a dense population of hermits!

Pete's interest had been aroused during his previous stay at Tamanrasset, when he had made the acquaintance of one of the ex-hermits, an Englishman. From this man he learned that the hermits, for the most part, came to Taza to study some branch or other of the occult (moon-worship, it seems, was a speciality) and the practitioners claimed that favourable conditions for their studies prevailed on this mountain. Some form of radiation, it was alleged, emanated from the ground there. The notion of emanations from Taza was, apparently, not a new one confined to these recent students: later on in Tamanrasset we heard stories of tribesmen in past ages who heard voices coming from the mountain that warned, guided or prophesied.

Research teams were reported to have located uranium deposits at Taza.

On the slopes of the mountain I came across two neatly built stone altars. Pete told me they were altars of the moon-worshippers that had been described to him. On the flat top of the mountain were what I took to be ancient tombs: there were several of these and they were all of the same odd shape,

something like an arrow head, outlined by large stones, and pointing in the same direction. One of the stories we were told concerned these tomb-like stones. In days long past, when brigands hid in these hills to waylay camel caravans crossing the Sahara, Taza was a special hideout. Old women would lie down on these sites and press their ears to the ground. From the ground they would hear messages concerning approaching caravans and their routes and movements. How these stories originated I have no idea.

The mountain was crowned by a small stone-built chapel. This had lately been consecrated by the monks of the order founded by Père de Foucauld and they had dedicated it to *Notre Dame de Confiance*, words written on the building. Previously it had been dedicated to some less holy power.

One of the hermits (the Englishman Pete had met) had slept in this chapel for a time, but had been forced to vacate it as snakes, of which there were many on Taza, were inclined to share the hermit's bed with him. When this happened, the hermit was obliged to lie motionless until such time as his uninvited bedfellow decided to move off of its own accord. At last the hermit decided he could stand it no longer and built himself a new house (actually two little buildings, which might be designated bed-sitting room and kitchenette). His new abode was on the mountainside where the rock was too sheer above and below to permit such visitations. We identified it on the slope above the well and the two tiny constructions feature in one of my paintings.

On our first night at Taza a full moon rose over the shoulder of the hill facing the moon-worshippers' altars; it was almost more like sun than moon, shedding a light so intense that we both instinctively sought to shelter for the night in the rice-and-sugar house that was so conveniently situated near the car. In the middle of the night I was disturbed by Pete, who seemed to be making quite a commotion.

"Wake up, wake up. There's something moving in the house."

His voice held a note of urgency seldom heard. I was deeply asleep, but the significance of the remark was clear even as I struggled to the surface. We reached for a torch and played it round the low stone shelf that surrounded the walls a couple of feet above floor-level. In one corner, crouching in fear, was a furry desert rat with a long brown bushy tail. Normally I was not too keen on rats, but this one seemed so innocuous in comparison with other creatures of the mountain that I took quite a liking to it. I turned over and went to sleep again.

Albeit, the next night we slept in the sand of the *oued* under efficient moon defences and well removed from smooth rock surfaces where slithery things are wont to slither.

❦

I can report nothing concerning our stay at Taza that will add anything to the annals of psychical research. But if there are places that have an uncanny atmosphere attached to them, then I think that Taza is such a place.

CHAPTER TWENTY-TWO

Life in the Hoggar Mountains

> For you see, so many out-of-the-way things had happened lately, that Alice had begun to think that very few things indeed were really impossible.
>
> *Alice's Adventures in Wonderland*

We were feeling that we'd learned to live with intermittent car trouble. A new dilemma confronted us now in which we had to face a period with a car in a permanent state of malaise.

Could the answer be camels? After some deliberation we knew they'd never do. Camels take twenty-one days to cover the same ground that a truck does in twelve hours. Picturesque, yes, but not for us while we wanted to get around as much as possible in a limited time. The time factor apart, we needed our transport to serve also as our house.

So it was that we continued to use the ailing car. However, we did go to great lengths to invent all sorts of safety devices – laughable, maybe, to read about. But they worked!

Such devices included the affixing of old tyres to the rear corners of the car to save the bodywork should we have to roll back into rocks; or towing a heavy stone a few inches behind a wheel – invaluable in the event of stalling on some kinds of upward gradient.

Our driving techniques, already skilled to cope with the vagaries of this car – no synchromesh on first gear meant double declutching – needed even further polishing. Use of the handbrake became vital, as did super-nimble steering.

The loss of power was due to a burnt-out valve. To lighten the load, one of us usually walked on upward slopes, leaving the other to drive alone to the top and then wait – tedious, but beneficial for the engine, giving it a chance to cool. When a passenger, I occasionally held the door ajar, ready to jump out; but I was not too keen on this practice!

On at least one occasion, when the situation seemed desperate, we unloaded the entire cargo and carried it uphill by hand; the car could then just make it to the top.

These are but some examples of the strategies that enabled us to keep going. The down side was the inordinate time it sometimes took to complete a short journey.

Not to be overlooked was something that occurred during an unexpected recurrence of tyre trouble. Away from our base camp one day, we were having a meal beside the car when we saw what looked like a hideous blister: a piece of inner tube protruded through a hole that had suddenly appeared in one of the tyres. By now I was becoming quite good at devising weird, outlandish remedies that lay beyond the realm of orthodox repair work, and I took over. I cut an old, unserviceable inner tube into strips to form a "bandage". This I wound round and round the tyre.

My cunning tourniquet was most effective, as it enabled us to drive the five miles back to base. Still intact on arrival, it looked so impressive that Pete took a photograph of the wheel with bandage in all its artistry. A print of this takes pride of place in my album.

One day we set out to explore the central range of the Hoggar, known as the Atakor. The size of Spain, it's a region of phonolytic peaks, the chimneys of ancient volcanoes, many of them rising 1,500 feet and more from their bases and sculpted by wind erosion. We saw a landscape that was as black and shiny as coal as far as the eye could see, and others where rock was highly coloured.

As we left Tamanrasset that day Pete had a furtive air that puzzled me. At the same time I noticed some unusual cargo with the load on the back – a mysterious small crate of half a dozen bottles. What were they, I wondered, and why had Pete covered them up in such a stealthy way?

We had not gone very far along the road, when Pete thought the time had come to divulge his secret. He cleared his throat and assumed a business-like manner, which overlaid the furtiveness that I had noticed earlier. He feared, he explained, that we might be stranded in the mountains (a fear hardly to be wondered at and one that I certainly shared) and therefore he planned to conceal bottles of water at strategic intervals along the way – lifesavers should he have to walk back to Tamanrasset in an emergency. Whenever a bottle was deposited, the location was charted on a map. This to me was nothing if not sound common sense – in fact it was a very wise thing to do. Nevertheless, Pete made me promise not to talk about it to any of our Tamanrasset friends.

On this trip we did break down, but the trouble was cured when Pete opened up the engine and replaced a valve. This extensive work was carried out while we camped on the slopes of the Asekrem, a great dome of a mountain rising to about 9,000 feet. This was an occasion when, stumped for want of a

certain tool required in the valve-changing operation, Pete set to and manufactured the tool on the spot before beginning to carry out the repair on the engine.

The water bottles? They may be lying to this day under Hoggar rocks lining the Boy Scout walk that never had to be walked.

We visited the summer hermitage of Père de Foucauld high on the Asakrem mountain. There we found two monks, followers of the renowned French monk who lived among the Tuareg up to the time of his assassination in 1916. The monks were dressed like Tuareg. We had supper with them, sitting cross-legged on the floor, a meal of soup and circular loaves of flat heavy bread. While we were eating, a ragged old Tuareg came to the door asking for some medical help and was invited to join us at the meal.

We saw the monks several times during the following few days. Père Jean-Marie made daily meteorological observations for the centre in Tamanrasset and on one occasion we accompanied him when he went to take his readings on the windy heights of the mountain, where his instruments were installed.

We learned from the monks that there were nuns somewhere in the vicinity, also living as Tuareg and herding goats. It was implied that they were not enthusiastic about receiving visitors, but nonetheless we decided to look them up.

Coming across a ravine with a well, we guessed that they must be somewhere near, but even then we didn't find them easily; they had found an extremely well concealed little hollow for their encampment. Finally, the barking of their dogs gave away their whereabouts. They made the best of it when they saw us coming, gave us a cordial welcome, and the sister in charge, a highly educated woman, showed us round the large camp. There must have been about twenty nuns and, like the monks, they wore Tuareg clothing. Normally, their only visitors were the monks, who trekked over the mountains to celebrate Mass in the tent they used as a church. Their camp suggested an authentic Tuareg way of life, though my tactless eye did fall on some packets of Knorr soup on the shelf!

At this altitude, where in winter there is sometimes ice on one's water-buckets and even snow is not unknown, we felt cold at night. The monks lent us each a floor-length wool bernous (cloak); these were so nice to wear that we hated having to give them back.

One day we were invited to a genuine Tuareg meal, when we visited a camp that we had espied on a hillside. The camp consisted of goatskin tents dyed the usual orange-red, and Tuareg women were sitting around outside the tents working with dyed skins to produce the decorative leatherwork I'd seen on saddles and sheaths and handles of swords. In view of the fact that the nobility do not normally work, they were probably Imrads, or vassals. Tuareg men forge the blades of these double-edged swords. In the old days they used metal mined in the Sahara for this; at this time they were using old car springs or other scrap metal.

Also in the camp were a few Tuareg slaves, and near the women lay a young goat. We understood that the goat had been attacked by a hyena and was being nursed in the camp until it was fit enough to rejoin the flock. I spent a couple of hours on a painting of the camp, and was glad to have an excuse for not sharing in the meal. Pete ate everything he was offered, pronouncing it good, but then he was less sensitive than I when it came to eating unidentifiable delicacies.

The Ilamane peak is the focal point of this region. It towers majestically above a great horseshoe-shaped valley, where we found lots to explore. There were tiers of rocks in the shape of organ pipes. We found the shapes and differing colours quite stunning as we came upon tier after fantastic tier. There were graves of French soldiers who were killed in ambush when General Laperrine was striving to make the Sahara caravan-route safe in the early part of the twentieth century. It was easy to imagine how the rocks provided perfect cover for those lying in wait as the soldiers advanced up the valley. There was one hill composed entirely of polygonal columns similar to those found at the Giant's Causeway in Northern Ireland. Further on, a long and colourful camel caravan was winding its way through the valley, a spectacle seemingly too good to be true.

We walked for some hours up a narrow winding *oued*. The monks had tipped us off about this, saying it was the most beautiful "nature's garden"; they were right, the further we walked the more marvellous it became. I thought of Delius's music *A Walk to the Paradise Garden*.

While in this valley we drove over a rocky road, at one point of which a few yards were striped with all the colours of the rainbow.

In my quest for a "lunar landscape", the Atakor was unrivalled. I was rewarded here with what has been referred to as a "lunar continent"!

CHAPTER TWENTY-THREE

Tamanrasset – personalities and events

The Queen had only one way of settling all difficulties, great or small. "Off with his head!" she said, without even looking round.

Alice's Adventures in Wonderland

It was on the wall of a little stone refuge where we lodged on the Asakrem that I spotted a scorpion as I entered. It was the second and last scorpion encountered on our journey. The first had been promenading on the sand in Agadès a few inches from where I sat myself down. On each occasion one of us killed the creature without difficulty.

Not so easy to dispatch was an objectionable snake encountered about this time. After a few days at the Tamanrasset hotel, when the thrill of baths and French cuisine had worn off, we started sleeping in the open again. We'd come to a stage when there was something physiologically irksome about sleeping hemmed in by walls; even if cost had been no object, we still preferred to sleep under the stars. We chose for our campsite an attractive spot set among a group of smooth rocks, the latter providing good natural props for my moon defences.

Coming "home" one evening, we found the site already occupied – by a large and lively snake that wriggled about in the sleeping quarters. Pete had an axe among his tools and with this he went for the snake. Blow followed blow and I was reluctant to look, especially as the creature seemed immune to killing, like Rasputin. It was quite uncanny. When at long last it seemed certain that the snake was dead, Pete gave two terrific blows for good measure and then left the body where it lay on a flat-topped rock. We turned our backs and started to prepare our food to take our minds off the incident. Some minutes later I looked round. To my alarm, the rock on which the snake had lain was bare; then I saw Rasputin on the sand nearby. Pete took the body away on the shovel and I never saw it again – to my relief!

When we described the snake to friends, we were told that it was of the most dangerous variety. We never again felt drawn to our attractive campsite. After all, one has relatives.

Just before dusk one evening, a very harmless visitor approached us, a natural friendliness and curiosity overcoming shyness. It was a dainty little gazelle. I spoke to it. It replied. I imitated. It liked this and came closer, continuing to utter its own noises so long as I imitated each time. The gazelle and I kept this up for minutes, while Pete listened with astonishment. It was queer to think that friendly, gentle creatures like this were targets for the guns of some of our Tamanrasset friends; men who, after a "successful" day's hunting, proudly posed for the camera in that horrid style of bygone days, gun in hand, foot resting on body of victim.

❦

"And what do you have for meals?" asked Mrs Barnett.

The Barnetts, a Protestant missionary couple, were interested to know more about our way of life.

"Well, she makes excellent pancakes..."

"*Pancakes*? But they need eggs!"

"Oh, she makes them without eggs!"

No cook by nature, but liking good food, I had occasionally tried out new dishes, some of which were successful enough to be in regular demand thereafter. Among these were the so-called "pancakes". I found that an eggless batter of flour and tinned milk could be fried without sticking when poured onto a very hot pan of boiling Vegetaline (the brand name of our cooking fat). A filling was folded in during cooking, usually corned beef. What resulted was something like a cross between cannelloni or ravioli and pancake.

So touched was the generous Mrs Barnett when she thought about the eggless pancakes that she straightaway took from her store cupboard a packet of American dried egg powder to present to us. Pancakes became more popular than ever after that.

Someone found among the elusive Tuareg one man who was willing to pose for a portrait. He arrived arrayed in the fabulous Tuareg gala costume that was becoming increasingly rare. It was made of a special indigo-coloured material that shimmers like carbon paper. The Tuareg obtained this material in the western Sudan to the south of Timbuktu. It was very expensive and they had always paid for it with a number of goats. The merchants had started to demand money, which the Tuareg did not have, and for this reason the costume was apparently dying out.

Madame Dufour, the wife of an official of the Tamanrasset administration, offered the use of her verandah for the sitting. All went well and I completed the work with exceptional speed – two large eyes and the bridge of a nose and for the rest just draperies. The next invitees for sittings I found myself. The fact that they were females at large in the town meant they were prostitutes; any other women would have been hidden away behind locked doors. Madame Dufour, with admirable breadth of mind, assured me she would not object on account of their calling, and I continued to use her verandah for sittings. My two models, Alamiya and Hadusha, were nothing like the vicious looking Ouled Naïls whom I saw in the whore quarters of El Goléa, further north. They were beautiful, happy-looking and delightful people. One could not but admire

1   Hadusha, Tamanrasset. A painting in oils.
2   Mount Taza. Entry to a hermit's dwelling.
    A painting in gouache.

Paintings in gouache.
3 Mosque in Agadès.
4 Wayside village.

Paintings in gouache.
5 *Weaving at Poli.*
6 *Ngaoundéré.*

7 Olivia and the
pick-up truck
among rocks north
of In Guezzam.

8 Olivia among
columnar rocks,
Hoggar
Mountains.

9 Olivia in the Hoggar Mountains.

10 Olivia seated on the motor cycle, now abandoned, used by Pete on his earlier Sahara crossing.

11 Woman in Poli.

12 Spectators at the gun-dance, Babanki-Tonga.

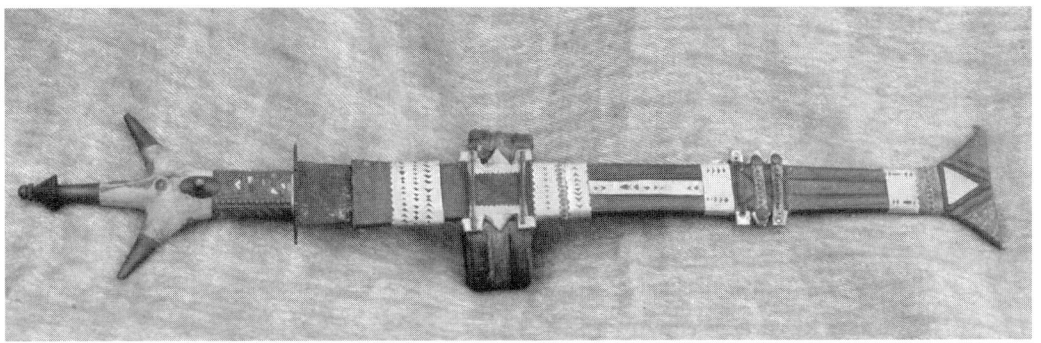

13 Banyo.
14 Ceremonial sword worn on the arm in a leather sheath
by the Tuareg.

15 Spinning and weaving in Houmsiki.
16 Tuareg in their tent.

them. As to their profession, if a woman wanted independence and freedom in their society, there was no choice; no other profession was open to women; it was that or a life of imprisonment.

Hadusha was young and had the angelic expression of a Madonna. Alamiya was getting on in years, very tall and had a great hawk-like nose that went with her dignified bearing. She was positively regal.

When Hadusha came to pose she brought with her a girl friend for company. While I worked the two sat side-by-side mumbling and giggling together. During the sitting, to appear friendly, I made an attempt at conversation. I had been told that Hadusha had recently got married. I asked her if that was so. Hadusha smiled ingenuously as she said she wasn't married, she was a prostitute – "Non, je suis putain." She spoke with a candour that was quite disconcerting.

The afternoon wore on and the portrait was nearing completion when the companion came over to me and explained that Hadusha was feeling restive and "it was her time for starting work." I managed to finish the portrait within a few minutes and I hoped that Hadusha would be on time in starting her night's work.

The magnificent Alamiya invited us to a tea party at her little house. The fact that her French was almost as non-existent as our Arabic was no real hindrance. There was Pete's accomplishment of being able to surmount language barriers; and she had also invited a young French-speaking boy to help things along. While Alamiya made tea the boy handed round cigarettes. These he lit for us with matches struck on the soles of his bare feet.

Alamiya's brew of green mint tea contained such quantities of sugar that I had difficulty in swallowing any. But I knew that politeness demanded that a guest drink at least three cupfuls, and I did succeed in gulping it down somehow.

Alamiya was a person of great character, gracious and charming. As we were leaving, she generously gave me one of her bead bracelets as a present.

❦

Living alone in a tiny house close to Alamiya's was an Englishwoman, Daisy Wakefield. Now very elderly, Miss Wakefield had settled down to end her days in Tamanrasset and was devoting all her time and energies to the task of translating the Bible into the Tuareg language. (Tuareg have their own script, called *tifinag*.) She was one of that breed of Englishwomen who chose to leave home and a normal way of life to spend years in an alien environment. Daisy Wakefield had spent much of her life doing missionary work among the Arabs. I once recognised her as she was drawing water from a well, an unmistakable figure, small and spare, and dressed in the Bedouin garments she habitually wore. Unfortunately I never met her personally, but she was certainly a well-known personality in Tamanrasset.

❦

One of our favourite spots in the region was a natural reservoir of water known as a *guelta*. At several different levels on a rocky precipice were pools of crystal-clear water, with rivulets descending vertically from one to the other. The lowest pool was greenish and was the habitat of a thousand frogs. A climb of a few feet brought one to the edge of the most idyllic rock swimming pool, and here the water was blue. Thereafter climbing became difficult, but rewarding. At a higher level a most unexpected oleander tree overhung the pool; it was ablaze with blossom when I saw it. We became familiar with the drive to this spot, and the car could tackle it without risk.

People living in Tamanrasset did not generally have cars and the Dufour family were delighted to come with us when we invited them on a swimming and picnic outing to this *guelta*. They enjoyed themselves enormously, afterwards wanting to go further afield – "the drive was so exciting." Little did they know how exciting it was for me with my undisclosed knowledge about the brakes. Monsieur Dufour and I, perched on the back, were tossed about like two peas in a drum while Pete, at the wheel, seemed to be heading homeward at a slightly uncalled-for speed, perhaps intent on getting the ordeal over quickly.

"How well suited your car is to mountain conditions," remarked Monsieur Dufour apropos of nothing, as we tried to hold fast to our seats. I found it difficult to agree – still more so to imagine the condition of a car that was ill-suited to them.

❦

When the day's work is done, there are few diversions in a place like Tamanrasset. Conversation is probably the main one – conversation and the exchange of stories when the men congregate to enjoy their aperitif, the ubiquitous *anisette*.

Monsieur and Madame Aubert were just back from leave in Algiers and it was the distressing misadventure that befell Madame Aubert's new coat during their leave that provided an anecdote currently being passed around and provoking lots of laughter. Poor Madame Aubert!

Madame Aubert was delighted with her new coat – I believe it was a Paris model. Needing to buy some shoes and other accessories to match it, she wore the new coat on her next shopping expedition into town. At the best of times Algiers' trams tend to be overcrowded. But by the time Madame Aubert had finished in the shops it was rush-hour and she found herself on a tightly packed tram; not a seat anywhere was available and she had to stand. The crush was enough to crease and crumple her clothes, and she wished she'd taken a taxi.

More and more people crowded on until she was completely wedged, unable to move. The extreme proximity of those around became quite unpleasant. An Arab, complete with flowing white robes, was pressed against her, but she could not withdraw one centimetre; she merely managed to clutch her handbag very tight and swivel round a fraction, thus avoiding the embarrassment of being almost cheek to cheek with the Arab as he breathed down her neck.

The tram jolted along, the tightly pressed passengers jostled and rocked, as it made its way to the outskirts of the town.

How pleasant to emerge into the fresh air again! thought Madame Aubert, as the tram drew to a halt and the time had come at last to alight.

The journey had been trying enough. It was only after she eventually stepped down to the pavement, however, that a downward glance at her coat revealed the full story of the jostling on the tram.

Chapter Twenty-four

More about food

Serve up in a clean dish, and throw the whole out of the window as fast as possible.

Edward Lear, "To Make an Amblongus Pie"

Pete's interest in food made him a keen shopper. On one or two occasions we happened to see a goat being led to the marketplace, and we knew what its fate was to be. Where fridges are unknown, it is customary to slaughter the animal and cut it up at once on the spot. Whenever Pete saw this possibility of buying fresh meat, he hurried round to join the circle of waiting customers.

On one occasion he bought an extra quantity of meat. "I'm going to dry it," he said, "lots of people preserve it by drying it in the sun." Personally I suspected that there was more to it than that, though I knew nothing about the process called "jerking". Pete, however, seemed quite confident, rubbing the meat with salt and putting it to hang out of the car window all day. In this, his confidence was quite misplaced. It got smelly in no time and after a few days the stink was so terrible that my insistence on digging a deep hole and burying the horrid, curling object met with no resistance.

We had trouble with vegetables too. Once we had no onions and Pete bought a bagful of an unfamiliar onion-like vegetable. Neither of us knew what they were, but I chopped up a good half dozen for our evening stew-pot in the hope they'd be nice. The stew was very tasty. The "onions" were garlic!

Pete was always on for trying new recipes, but unfortunately they were not invariably successes. There were one or two dismal failures that may be worthy of mention. Saharan macaroni cheese was an especially striking failure.

Pete had never heard of macaroni cheese. I warned him that a proper one required an oven and also that I had no idea of the recipe, so it would have to be a complete shot in the dark. He was nevertheless keen to sample a dish that is not known in Holland.

I first made a sauce, blending flour and watered-down milk and adding a rather dried up piece of cheese, after first shredding it. I then boiled the mixture, stirring carefully so that there were no lumps, but by the time it was cooked it had a distinctly pasty consistency, and looked really more suited for use by a paper-hanger than anything else. When the macaroni was cooked I drained it and added the cheese sauce. The result was unspeakable; the macaroni (itself by definition a "wheaten paste") and my paste-like floury sauce combined to make a gooey mess that literally stuck in the gullet.

Pete decided against introducing macaroni cheese into Holland.

Another disappointment was unfortunately a dish intended as a treat. We both had birthdays while at Tamanrasset, events that we regarded as important. My treat day came first, as I was three weeks older (a fact that sometimes made me feel bossy).

In the morning Pete bought me a present of a box of chocolates (the most expensive I had ever eaten) and this was not such a mad choice as it sounds, as that day we were heading for the mountains where it was cool enough to keep chocolates in good condition. They were of course not required to keep for very long. As well as the chocolate, I was relieved of all kitchen duties for twenty-four hours; a very rare treat.

When Pete's birthday came round, he made his own choice of present. He liked offal, a taste that I do not share. So much do I dislike it that I don't even care to handle the stuff. However, he said he wanted kidneys, so as a birthday treat I agreed to cook the nasty-looking objects in the parcel he was seen to be clutching half an hour after a pretty little goat was dragged into the market.

"I *am* looking forward to them," said Pete, suddenly quite a gourmet. "They'll be delicious so fresh, and it's months since I tasted kidneys."

The task of frying them was really not so bad and the anticipation of the pleasure they were going to give made it worthwhile anyway. When done to a turn they looked quite appetising, even to me, and I almost felt I could sample one myself. However, they were Pete's special treat so I contented myself with sitting to watch his enjoyment.

He seized his knife and fork. He savoured the first mouthful and I awaited a paean of praise for my cooking.

"Ugh!" said Pete, his expression turning to one of anything but enjoyment. He pushed his plate onto a rock behind him and stretched for a biscuit to take away the taste.

"I'm sure I cooked them perfectly," I said in amazement.

"It's not the cooking," he said, his face still distorted as though I had given him something unfit for human consumption.

"What is it then? What did they taste of?"

He kept shuddering at the recollection of the taste, while continuing to mutter "Ugh!"

For quite some time I could get nothing out of him by way of reply. Then at long last I got the answer.

"Urine," said Pete.

Quite possibly macaroni cheese did exist in Holland but was not identifiable with my Saharan variety. I think it's safe to assume, however, that birthday kidneys are served in no country in the world.

Both the Auberts and the Dufours invited us to dinner, providing meals that were a delightful contrast to the ones just described. Tremendous gastronomic feasts were prepared in our honour.

At the Dufours' a special treat had been arranged. We knew about it, as we had called at their house during the morning and the secret had been confided to us. A home-made nut ice-cream was about to be put into the freezer. It was made to a special recipe provided by a neighbour, and the neighbour herself was with Madame Dufour to supervise and help in the preparation. This was obviously to be the highlight of the evening.

The dinner was all we expected it to be – and more. One or two other guests had been invited to meet us, one of them the distinguished-looking and charming Monsieur Gerard, about whom I was to learn more later on.

Course followed course. Having a fairly good digestion, I sampled them all. Pete, who had the digestion of an ox, was doing even better, accepting helping after helping.

The dinner Madame Lambert gave us in Nkongsamba may have been lacking in sweet courses, but Madame Dufour's was not; there were several. First, before the special nut ice-cream, each person was served with a miniature rice mould, chilled. Although I would be at pains to find fault with any of the other courses, the rice in this dish was unfortunately under-cooked, which resulted in the grains being hard at the centre and difficult to chew.

After the first spoonful or two, Pete jumped to the conclusion that this was the celebrated nut ice-cream. Eager to show his appreciation of our hostess's efforts, he repeatedly interrupted the conversation to comment on the pudding.

"Really delicious, this nut ice," he kept saying, crunching the hard grains between his teeth. "I do congratulate you on its success."

I made one attempt to kick him lightly on the shin. This only caused him to peer under the table to see if Chiffon, the spaniel, had crept in and was nudging him, before continuing to extol the excellence of the pudding.

When the nut ice-cream really did come, Pete, believing his duty as an appreciative guest to be fulfilled, became engrossed in conversation. The mixture contained nuts that were finely ground and he was unaware of what exactly he was eating.

❦

The parts having at last arrived, the brakes were repaired and we began to think about our onward journey.

Chapter Twenty-five

Tamanrasset – more personalities and events

"Curiouser and curiouser!" cried Alice.

Alice's Adventures in Wonderland

Monsieur Gerard was the distinguished-looking man we'd met at dinner at the Dufours'. He was blue-eyed and wore a goatee. The Touring Club de France brought small groups of people by air from Paris, and Monsieur Gerard's job was to drive them round the mountainous region, the Atakor, in his specially fitted jeep. It was too hot now for visitors, and he was thus preparing to leave for Algiers with his jeep.

When in Tamanrasset previously, Pete had formed a slight acquaintance with Monsieur Gerard. He now asked me what impression I had of him. I said that, from what I'd seen of him and the few words we'd exchanged, I judged him to be an intelligent and civilised man.

It must have crossed the minds of several people that here was a suitable opportunity for us to continue our journey speedily and in comfort; and, if we were to accompany Monsieur Gerard on his trip north, we should, we imagined, constitute quite a congenial party. Disposing of the Morris should not be difficult in Tamanrasset; its good appearance appealed to the Arab merchants, some of whom were already eyeing it with interest. It all seemed to add up to a good idea.

It was Madame Dufour who put the suggestion forward on our behalf. Yes, Monsieur Gerard was interested, she told us, and he would come round to the hotel, where we were staying at the time, to discuss the idea.

He duly arrived. I happened to be out and he got hold of Pete. Coming straight to the point, he would, he said, certainly enjoy having companionship on the trip to Algiers and would offer us the opportunity of going with him – but on one condition. The condition? "That we share the *Anglaise*." He paused, waiting for some reaction, but Pete was too taken aback to speak, even wondering if he'd heard aright.

"Think it over," said Monsieur Gerard at last, "and if you agree to my terms, come round to my house tomorrow evening." Then he was gone, leaving Pete still in a bemused state – which is how I found him when I got back.

Pete was now thinking that there must have been something in the nature of flirtation that he hadn't noticed between Monsieur Gerard and me. "You never mentioned anything," he said. "At least the man must have got a wrong impression; perhaps that time you sat next to him at the Dufours."

"It's preposterous," I said, almost past speech. I cast my mind back to that party. I'd been my usual rather quiet self, friendly but very decorous, choosing my words with care. It was a style I had come to adopt most rigorously at these social gatherings in an attempt to avert any unfortunate misinterpretations. "Oh dear, one just can't win," I thought.

We never saw the "civilised" Monsieur Gerard again.

❦

Supply routes for Tamanrasset were to the north, where the *piste* was kept open the whole year round and did not present anything like the same dangers as the section we had left behind. Yet, ironically, we were not now allowed to proceed except in convoy. We would have been happy to set off on our own, which goes to show how foolhardy we must have become. Arab trucks drive fast, and we needed a leisurely pace for reasons of both necessity and inclination. In addition, truck owners were always reluctant to be bothered with escorting tourist cars, which they were meant to keep in view at all times.

It was with some relief that we heard that one Ben Nasser, a wealthy merchant, was prepared to discuss the matter with us.

We had coffee with him at his house. I was sorry I had thought it necessary to accompany Pete. Ben arranged to sit next to me. My mind was focused on the problems in hand; while Ben, too, had a problem – his was how to control how his hand was occupied. How impossible it seemed to have any normal "man-to-man" contacts in these regions if I was involved!

The full story unfolded. Ben had a brother. The brother had several wives. The wives were in Tamanrasset, but he wanted them transported to In Salah, the next oasis on the road north. Such a passenger list naturally created problems. But if we were drawn into the picture, thought Ben, a ready-made solution might be to hand; for he had noticed that the back of our pick-up truck, if well walled in with tarpaulins, could provide reasonable accommodation for the ladies. At first glance it looked as though something might be worked out. But, the more one examined the situation, the more complex it began to look.

Although he couldn't sit with them, it was nevertheless mandatory that Ben travel in the same vehicle as his sisters-in-law. Pete could not sit with them either. I, it seemed, was the only member of the party who could. When I thought about it, though, I couldn't take to the idea of being boxed in and joggled for all the 427 miles to In Salah. Nor did Pete fancy the idea of driving that distance without relief. Could we all three sit in the front? I was reluctant to be closeted next to Ben (he of the wandering hand). Thus, if we were to squash three into the front, Pete would have to be a buffer, sandwiched in the middle, and I'd have to drive without a break. By now the problem had begun to look like the fox-and-geese puzzle, but without a solution.

Finally, we said that we considered transporting so many would make us overweight, and it would not be convenient to put any of our stuff on the truck. Ben accepted this with a good grace, saying we could go with them in convoy anyway. A major work was then embarked on to adapt the big truck to suit requirements, and soon the arrangements for an early departure were confirmed.

"After Monsieur Gerard and his proposition, one begins to wonder what next," I remarked. Next was Monsieur Martin and *his* proposition. We knew Monsieur Martin well by sight, having noticed him at the hotel since our first arrival in Tamanrasset. He was middle-aged, well turned out and solidly built; one could say he looked a solid man in every sense. We once exchanged a few words with him, at which time he'd told us that he was a consultant, mentioning a well-known French company. We wondered vaguely why his job necessitated such a lengthy sojourn in a place like this, but it wasn't our affair and we didn't question him. I thought he might perhaps be in semi-retirement and busy writing a book, or something like that, for we never met him outside the hotel. He always kept himself very much to himself and seldom seemed to chat with fellow-guests. He's a bore, I decided, for local inhabitants seemed to steer clear of him.

A bore he might be, but Monsieur Martin approached us with a pleasant enough manner. It had reached his ears that we were contemplating selling the car. He was eager, he said, to purchase a car here in the Sahara and, as he might have to wait some time before another opportunity arose, would we consider an offer? Yes, he knew the car had shortcomings, but he'd made up his mind he wanted it nonetheless.

Price was obviously not an important consideration for Monsieur Martin. He wanted to tempt us and he therefore offered a decent sum.

Someone connected with his company was at In Salah, he told us, and was holding funds for him. He suggested that, to avoid delaying the purchase, we might perhaps give him a lift to In Salah, where the deal could go ahead.

It sounded a fair enough proposition. The feeling stayed with us that we could never have enough of the desert: on the other hand, there was no doubt that we'd had more than enough of the car. It would be quite possible to find some means to make our way onwards from In Salah.

"That Monsieur Martin wants to buy the car," remarked Pete to his friend Monsieur Aubert. "Seems a good chance for us, though we must take him to In Salah, where it seems he has funds awaiting him." Monsieur Aubert looked uncertain, but said nothing.

First thing next morning, a member of the administration rushed round to see us. They had just received confirmation of suspicions they already had about Monsieur Martin's true identity. He was wanted in connection with a criminal offence and now his arrest was imminent.

Had it not been for Pete's chance remark and Monsieur Aubert's quick action, this man might have succeeded in slipping away and perhaps out of the country, with our unwitting cooperation. At all events, our hopes of a sale were dashed sooner rather than later.

❦

We duly left Tamanrasset. It was well into June, when Sahara temperatures were soaring. Even so, we seemed to take the mounting heat in our stride, which goes to show how well, given enough time, human beings can become acclimatised to things.

Pete had explained to the Arab party the need for not straining our car and on the road they were considerate towards us, breaking rules by allowing us a head start each morning. But what further saved the situation was prayer.

Prayer time came round with blessed frequency. When it did, for a precious half hour or more we could relax from the strain of keeping up the unaccustomed pace, and our engine could have a chance to cool. The white-clad occupants of the truck would descend and take up their prostrate positions, temples pressed to the sand.

A very young bride completely veiled from head to toe presented a sight I had not seen before. I saw her descending from the cabin of the truck, where she sat separated from the driver by a very old woman. The very old woman would herd all the wives together quickly and guide them to a retreat at a suitable distance, thirty yards or so away. For siesta, and at night, a large tent would be erected for them.

❦

Some catastrophe would surely befall us before our arrival at In Salah; we both somehow felt it instinctively. And we were not wrong. Late on the second evening, the Morris squealed and, with a gesture of seeming exhaustion, nose-dived towards the sand. Once again, it was the front offside of the car.

I jumped from the passenger seat and lowered my head to the sand. I peered under and upward. This was a part of the car's anatomy with which I was familiar; I was there at Douala when it was being modified, and I had witnessed the twisting of the torsion bars (which provided the suspension). This had been an effective means of raising the car so that it became higher off the ground. Now the sight of the tangled metal left me in no doubt as to what had happened. The fixture holding the right-hand torsion bar to the chassis had succumbed to stress, and wrenching itself clear, had ripped into shreds.

"It looks bad," I yelled to Pete. He looked bad; and I felt bad.

Our Arab friends were kindly and, as it was already getting late, they agreed to halt for the night. What feat of ingenuity could Pete now come up with to get us going again? With this thought, I fell asleep.

The next thing I knew I was being roused by Pete. "Quick," he was saying, "we must have breakfast and get on our way at once."

Our fellow-travellers were just beginning to stir, and above the eastern horizon the stars were merging into a pale blue glimmer of light. Bleary-eyed with sleep, but jolted into consciousness by recollections of the latest disaster, I peered at the car. Lo and behold, it seemed to be standing on an even keel again, all fair and square – indeed a fine-looking vehicle, ready for anything.

As I made breakfast, I listened to the recounting of the night's unceasing work. "I removed a shock-absorber, stuffed it full of sand, and then replaced it the other way up. It should see us through until we can get to a welder at In Salah."

My head reeled! I was well used to observing the bewildering resourcefulness Pete could muster in emergencies. But I've come to regard the upside-down, sand-filled shock-absorber episode as his *tour de force.* Had we been on an operation of war, he would surely have earned a medal that day.

We gobbled breakfast. Then, while the Arabs rubbed their eyes in disbelief, we zoomed away into the hills ahead.

"I'll drive," Pete had said. I could see he was pretty exhausted due to lack of sleep – and we had both been very tired the night before – but I didn't argue the point. It was obviously something to do with male pride and the presence of our observers.

❦

The sun was now rising behind a range of smooth, low hills crowned mile after mile with a ridge of rock that looked just like the ramparts of a fortress, doorways and all. The narrow road skirted a steep slope, veering to the right in a wide curve; at the left was an unprotected drop. Suddenly, instead of following the curve of the road, the car kept straight ahead towards the edge and the sheer drop. I grabbed the heavy steering wheel and succeeded in wrenching it round to the right. With scarcely a split second to spare, we swerved to follow again the course of the road. As I stretched over him, Pete gave a little jump; he had fallen asleep at the wheel.

I may not have had many chances to distinguish myself, but I think I can rightfully claim that this at last was my *tour de force.*

We stopped and prepared a bed in the joggly back, onto which Pete sank unprotesting. "I'm all in," he declared, for him a unique admission. And no amount of joggling prevented him from sleeping throughout the day.

It was difficult to drive very smoothly, on account of a petrol crisis. Something had occurred prior to the torsion-bar incident, which had involved some slight leakage of petrol. Pete had reminded me to conserve it, which entailed keeping in high gears, sometimes shuddering along in top or third when a change down would be desirable.

"You did see the stones with holes right through them like modern sculpture, didn't you?" asked Pete anxiously that evening. He had never forgotten those stones, which he had marked on his map when he had first seen them. I assured him that I had indeed seen them, but he was annoyed that he had not witnessed my delight at that event.

Chapter Twenty-six

In Salah

The crew was complete: it included...
A maker of Bonnets and Hoods...

The Hunting of the Snark

There was not very much in In Salah, and we didn't stay there long.

As usual we quickly made friends at the hotel, and some of these were oil company officials. One morning Pete was whisked away on his own to be shown the oilfields, and I looked forward to a day of relaxation on my own. As he walked in company with his hosts towards a waiting jeep, he was accosted in urgent fashion by a man whose acquaintance he had already made. "My dear fellow, do you mean to say you are leaving her alone?" was the gist of his exhortation. "The hotel is just not suitable; it is frequented by rough, tough types, truck drivers and so on!"

Pete thought no more about it, but on his return his first question was: "Did anyone bother you?" "Only one," I replied. "Everyone was decent, except that tall man they call Jean." I described how I had tried to sit in the shady little courtyard outside the bedrooms and this man had intruded, persistently admiring my suntan, an admiration that necessitated running his hands over my skin. "He was an absolute pest and in the end I had to shut myself into the room in all that heat."

Pete wore a puzzled frown while I was speaking. The man who had earlier denigrated the hotel clients was the tall man called Jean.

There were two Italian men there whom I remember on account of a conversation I had with one of them. They could speak French fluently, but it was with accents heavily overlaid with Italian. They liked to greet us in English and once or twice we returned the compliment with *Buon giorno* or *Arrivederci*.

One day one of the men came over and addressed me. Unable to understand floods of fluent Italian, I interrupted him with, "Could you speak in French, please?"

"I am speaking in French," said the man.

A sirocco blew, causing heat that made being indoors very trying, and everyone slept on the roof. We crept down before daybreak on the day of our departure to get in the maximum of driving before the heat of the day. We were no longer restricted to driving in convoy and it was pleasant to be on our own and set our pace as circumstance dictated.

A remarkable event occurred that morning after we had covered a very few miles. Suddenly what looked like a bird of gargantuan proportions swept before the windscreen and, with a faint swish, soared away overhead into the sky. We blinked and rubbed our eyes. The sun had not yet risen, but the dawn sky cast an opal light on the hills around us and this faint illumination revealed that our engine was unbonneted – naked. Pete walked back and retrieved the great bird from a hillside where it roosted, several hundred yards away. At first it didn't seem to fit at all, but I pieced it together and strapped it down in place with my clothesline.

That day we came to an abandoned car a few yards off the *piste* to our right. On the side were scrawled in big black letters the words "PRESS ON KEITH. THIS ISN'T US!" The Keith who had to press on was the Keith whom we'd met in Houmsiki, and the inscription dated from one of his earlier journeys when he had joined with friends, who drove in another car. His friends had got ahead and had left the message on the old wreck when their car was leading by a few miles. Keith had told us to look out for it!

This was the only abandoned car in over 1,200 miles of *piste*. Some years later I shuddered when I read that this desert route, which was the Trans-Sahara Highway of the future, was lined with countless abandoned wrecks and tyres.

CHAPTER TWENTY-SEVEN

Fort Miribel and El Goléa

This is rather sudden, Alice thought, but after such a *very* strong hint that she ought to be going, she felt that it would hardly be civil to stay.

Through the Looking-Glass

Fort Miribel lies between In Salah and El Goléa. It housed at that time some thirty or forty Frenchmen, employees of an oil company, as well as providing shelter for travellers of the *piste*. Water there was, but it was extremely salinated and, as I found to my cost, unfit for human consumption (though the map described it as drinking water). A very old man, who had once been a White Russian refugee, looked after the accommodation generally. He also kept a stock of refrigerated bottles containing water or other desirable liquids. The oil company provided their men with mineral water for drinking purposes and I noticed that they never drank from the water supply, understandable in view of its nasty taste.

❧

When I go on holiday in Europe it usually rains, even if it hasn't done so for ages. The night I arrived at Fort Miribel an unusual quantity of raindrops fell around us on the plateau of Tademaït. The old White Russian said there had been nothing like it in his thirty-two years in the Sahara.

Life for the men who lodged here was made up of six-week stints of duty interspersed with short trips to Algiers. All were now due, in a few days' time, to leave the Sahara for the hottest months, so presumably none had had leave very recently. Six weeks of celibacy had a telling effect at Fort Miribel, where nothing in the shape of a woman normally appeared. The old man knew: he regarded me with an apprehensive look and requested me not to pull my mattress outside at bedtime, as everyone did to ensure a tolerable night's sleep. Out of sight, out of mind was the principle. While I endured near suffocation within my four walls, I had a flesh-and-blood barricade: this was Pete, who lay like a fallen sentry outside my door.

I could suddenly no longer bear being indoors. When all was quiet, I crept out and lay down on Pete's mattress beside him, covering myself with a sheet. Just afterwards, I heard the sounds of a truck approaching and coming to a halt outside the fortress. As we were near the entrance, these late-night arrivals had more or less to step over us on their way in.

"Oh dear," I whispered, "they'll have seen two forms. What'll they make of it?"

"Homos," said Pete.

※

We had thought it opportune to stay for a few days at the fort, since interest in buying the Morris was being expressed by more than one prospective buyer. But there were indications that something else was stirring among the inhabitants: an outbreak of some kind of atavism. As the temperature mounted daily, so the atmosphere seemed to be increasingly charged in a subtle way. Whenever I walked around, there were manifestations of this that could by no means be described as subtle.

For example, a huge tank had been filled for use as a swimming pool. This was a blissful sight and, during the heat of the afternoon, when everyone was reported to be absent at their place of work, I climbed to the edge of the tank and plunged in. It was just too good to last. Some people were obviously more absent than others, for in no time I had company. Whether this consisted of one swimmer or more than one I cannot say. All I *can* say is that with me in the tank was an extraordinary species, all limbs like octopi. I had the sensation of limbs entwined and endlessly entangled with my own. With difficulty I shook them off at last. When extricated, I rose Aphrodite-like from the teeming water and fled.

Even showers were a problem. There was only one bathhouse and, let alone a door-lock, it hadn't even a door, as far as I can remember. A time was scheduled when I was told I would have the place to myself. "Now don't fuss," said Pete, afraid of being dragooned into standing guard. "I'm assured that all the men are absent."

There wasn't a soul to be seen anywhere as I entered the bathhouse, clutching my soap and towel. I turned on the shower and had just stepped under it when a most unnerving tableau was presented before my eyes. A muscular brown arm slid round the doorpost. There it remained, unmoving but for an index finger that curled upwards with beckoning motions. No body, no sound; there the story ends. Was it a figment of an overwrought imagination? The memory of the scene is vivid, so much so that whenever I think of Fort Miribel, I think of that vision round the doorpost.

It looked as if I were destined for dehydration: the water

was almost undrinkable, swimming was impossible, and now showering was out.

After a few such incidents, Pete was casually spreading the word around that I was an expert at judo. To serve the same purpose on some previous occasions he had indulged in a little chatter about the guns we carried, a device that had proved quite effective, especially if combined with a kind of jealous glint in the eye. The judo line now replaced this on account of the fact that arms and ammunition were prohibited on the *piste*.

Bleak and blazing hot, this was a place for an overnight stop and nothing more. So it was a relief when one of the young men, Georges, made up his mind and told us he definitely wanted to buy the car. It seemed expedient. We told Georges just how unfit the car had proved itself to be and made no secret of the great demands it had made on Pete to keep it going. Georges was not to be deterred; he obviously was mad keen to develop mechanical skills. "I'd enjoy tinkering at it," he declared, sounding almost a trifle envious of all that mass of activity of Pete's.

※

We had covered more than 3,000 miles since leaving Loum seven months previously, without counting many side-trips. It was strange how we were never disenchanted, and seemingly tireless. We had always hankered to see more and more – day-dreaming about possible diversions, to the very unexplored mountainous Aïre region perhaps, or to the prehistoric Tassili rock paintings. It was crystal clear that this was the time to draw the line and forget our fanaticism.

A modest price was agreed upon. Everyone was satisfied. Georges could have all the tinkering he could possibly desire, and would get fair value anyway with a large amount of good accessories and equipment that would be thrown in.

Up to this moment I had kept in rude health, apart from those few days of fever in Kano, and I'd got over that before the doctor could be sent for. Now I suddenly felt very off-colour, suffering from stomach pains and diarrhoea. I guessed what had stirred up the trouble: a passing truck-driver had given me a bottle of concentrated aniseed that disguised the foul taste of the salinated water, and I'd started drinking quite a bit.

The same day the shrewd old White Russian took Pete on one side and urged him to expedite our departure. Pete reported this to me as I lay in bed feeling worse hour by hour. "He says the men are going crazy and he cannot be responsible for anything that might happen."

"Well then, we must be considerate. I can be ready to take the next lift to El Goléa that we can get," said Marilyn Monroe, whom she now felt herself to be.

Pete sat in the doorway busily writing. "I'm trying to set down the entire list of mishaps with the car before they have faded from memory," he told me.

"Impossible," I cried, picturing a tome of the dimensions of *War and Peace*.

"Nothing too elaborate," replied Pete. "I want to write to Monsieur Bouvier in Douala. Not a letter of complaint, but he did ask me to let him know how we got on with the car, and I think he'd be interested to hear about it."

We began at the beginning and tried to think of the events as they had occurred, but soon realised that we could never remember details of all those mind-boggling catastrophes; so routine were they that they merged with those details of everyday life that get forgotten. So then we tried a better method: we went over the car bit by bit, like running through a manufacturer's manual, and this proved to be somewhat easier. Pete noted what he could remember of each component part. The conclusion was that the only part that had come through with impunity was the back axle.

The draft letter, as it progressed, made incredible reading. At the same time it was, unintentionally, awfully funny.

While I was laid up Pete remained on call to bring me cold drinks from the old man. "Please, a cold from the old," I murmured for the fifteenth time that day. "OK," said Pete, and he slipped the hilarious document into a book, which he tucked under his arm. While he was gone, he laid the book down somewhere. The men were starting to arrive back from work, and Georges, catching sight of a new book, idly picked it up.

A young man can be quite happy to have an old, well used car, even if it presents a challenge to his skill to keep it going. He does not feel so happy if he begins to see the car as an object of amusement.

Having read the document, Georges began to waver.

In the evening I felt able to rise from my sickbed. Putting on what I judged to be some un-sexy clothing – possibly an unnecessary measure considering my seedy appearance at the time – I joined the men for dinner. As I approached the table Pete was talking.

"Yes, it was an absurdly bad car they sold us. But now, after all, practically every single part has been repaired or renewed. Why, it's hardly the same car at all now!"

No one could argue the truth of that.

The car was sold and I felt no nostalgia at the parting. What Pete must have felt is beyond imagination.

We sorted through our things, picking out a few items we

valued to take with us, things like Madame Museau's coffee pot, which had served us so valiantly. Pete was most annoyed to find that there was now only one of the precious "Cameron clan" cufflinks that, flashy though they were, he'd kept among his valuables since buying them in Bamenda. He had become really attached to them.

One of the next travellers to arrive was a Frenchman in a heavy truck. He was leaving for El Goléa at an extremely early hour in the morning and, as he had space to spare, he agreed to take us with him. Our aim was to get to Algiers with minimum delay, and a radio message was sent reserving two seats on a flight leaving El Goléa at about lunchtime, which was judged to fit in well.

The truck was exceptionally uncomfortable and, to make matters worse, it was desperately slow.

This was all the more unfortunate as there were new effects from my drinking of the salinated water, and before we had got far in the slowcoach, I was feeling really ill, with an excruciating pain in the bladder. At the first stop I retrieved out of the packing the precious foam rubber cushion given to me as a parting present by Kathleen and Steve at Bota, and this did wonders to relieve the torture of the hard, vibrating seat.

I can't be sure how many hours it took us to rattle over the eighty-nine miles to El Goléa. It seemed interminable and every mile was a trial of endurance for me. Even when the strange emerald green hills of the oasis, a green caused not by vegetation but by coloured rock, came into view and I longed to reach them, they seemed like a mirage, never getting any nearer. For some miles there was a stretch of tarmac, laid experimentally, when the joggling lessened, but even this didn't seem to increase our speed perceptibly.

When I was beginning to think that we would never arrive, we did. We had missed the plane by a long way, and the truck dropped us at the hotel. We heard afterwards that Air France had delayed take-off for nearly an hour to wait for us.

❦

Horror of horrors – the last straw was yet to come. The hotel was full up, and the moment I had been dreaming of for so long was still not a reality. I looked around wildly, as though I hoped to see a luxurious bedroom materialising like a mirage. I caught sight of people sitting round a table in the courtyard and suddenly recognised them as a family we had already met in In Salah. So great was the change in my appearance that they scarcely recognised me.

The husband had been a Nazi SS man and the wife a French collaborator whom he had met during the war. We had heard it rumoured that they were being sought in connection with war crimes and were "on the run". Be that as it may, they were my greatest friends and allies that day. They were kindness itself, unhesitatingly giving me their room, which had the luxurious big bed I'd been dreaming of, and their little girl, whose name was Nicole, danced attendance on me till evening.

Nicole was an intelligent nine-year-old. The abnormal way of life, and being a child alone among adults, had made her seem old beyond her years. My being recumbent upstairs provided a pastime for the afternoon. She ran up and down regularly for the purpose of regaling me with snippets of the conversation taking place in the courtyard below. Nicole's mother was a brilliant *raconteuse* and Pete was drawing her out concerning some of her remarkable experiences in Algiers and the Sahara. Precocious as Nicole was, the import of some of the anecdotes was lost on her, and by the time they were relayed to me they were anything from very odd to quite incomprehensible.

Later on, after Pete had used his powers of persuasion on the hotel manager, it transpired that after all a room could be found, so all ended happily. My condition rapidly improved, and after a day or so and a couple of swims in the swimming pool overhung with red roses, whose beauty seemed to symbolise the sadness we were feeling, we left El Goléa, and the Sahara.

Chapter Twenty-eight

Algiers

"Begin at the beginning," the King said gravely, "and go on till you come to the end; then stop."

Alice's Adventures in Wonderland

The flight to Algiers was extraordinarily bumpy, with hardly any let-up during its three-hour duration; many passengers suffered from air-sickness, including Pete, who was badly stricken.

With this ordeal over, we got a taxi at the airport and asked to be taken to a comfortable and moderately priced hotel.

I was still convalescent and it showed in my appearance; Pete looked wan and haggard. With our battered luggage, we looked like a couple of down-and-outs. The French taxi driver took us to an area of cheap hotels that looked awfully dreary and uninviting; but they were, nonetheless, full up and we had to go from one to another. At a small hotel in a side street we felt we were lucky to be offered anything at all.

A woman showed us to our room. "That'll be 700 francs," she said, eyeing us suspiciously and remaining in the doorway. To get rid of her we handed her the money. As I closed the door I saw an official card stating the price to be 500. I re-opened the door, and we'd got rid of the woman all right –

she'd just vanished into thin air. The room was awful, quite poky, but full of furniture of a size (but not style) more suited to a baronial hall. There were numerous mirrors, and from certain points one could see hideous vases repeatedly reflected almost to infinity in facing pairs.

We felt hungry, but we'd already ascertained that there was no food at the hotel. We hurried out to find a restaurant. There was no curfew in force at that time, yet although it was only nine o'clock, the streets were completely deserted. We walked and walked but could find nothing open and not a soul to ask.

The sight of a door with a cheerful crack of light and the sound of bustle and voices brought a ray of hope to our feeling of despair. Inside we could see men at work in a bakery. We knocked, someone spoke to us through the crack, and to our relief the baker sold us two bagfuls of his leftover buns and cakes. As we hurried back to our hall of mirrors, the desolate streets echoed with our footsteps and the rustling of paper bags – we couldn't wait to broach our supper.

Our first evening in "civilisation" hadn't been a howling success.

❦

The next day we set out for the shops. We'd not got very far when we realised that my dress was causing a commotion. Pete learned from somebody in the crowd that had collected that the dress was "indecent". The trouble was that its bodice, though it came well up, finished under the armpits and had nothing over the shoulder. Apparently, although in Algiers necklines could – and did – plunge to great depths, there must be suspension over the shoulders to avoid a riot. I had to go back for a cardigan. Unaccustomed to shoes or pavements, our feet were getting rubbed and hurting.

At least my spirits rose when I bought some new clothes and found that smaller sizes now fitted me. Men's fashion had changed and Pete looked different in his new things. I kept failing to recognise him in the crowds.

Before we could begin to enjoy a meal, we were frozen to icebergs in the air-conditioned restaurant. The sirocco had arrived and Algiers was basking in a heat wave. People kept remarking, "What heat! Isn't it terrible?" while I genuinely thought it was pleasantly cool.

The boat to Marseilles was the next step.

"Let's go fourth class," said Pete airily. "Why waste money?"

I'd never heard of a fourth class. I wished later that I'd never *ever* heard of it, let alone discovered what it was like! Tough enough in some ways, I wasn't cut out for that.

Pete saw me off at the Marseilles station, before returning to Holland. I was heading for Geneva, hoping to find a job that might suit me. On the over-crowded, airless train I suffered greatly from the heat – stifling and oppressive almost beyond bearing.

It just wasn't *my* kind of heat!

Considering that the chapter of my life just ended had lasted nine months, seven of them spent in transit, I don't think that the process of re-adaptation to the next chapter took me too long. Life in Geneva, with all the trappings of civilisation, the international atmosphere and the chance of working in international organisations, had its compensations.

Still, the journey back from Bota was unforgettable and unforgotten (with apologies to Rupert Brooke).